Young Frankenstein

Paul Kain

Young Frankenstein

Olympia Publishers
London

www.olympiapublishers.com
OLYMPIA PAPERBACK EDITION

Copyright © Paul Kain 2024

The right of Paul Kain to be identified as author of this work has been asserted in accordance with sections 77 and 78 of the Copyright, Designs and Patents Act 1988.

All Rights Reserved

No reproduction, copy or transmission of this publication may be made without written permission.
No paragraph of this publication may be reproduced, copied or transmitted save with the written permission of the publisher, or in accordance with the provisions of the Copyright Act 1956 (as amended).

Any person who commits any unauthorised act in relation to this publication may be liable to criminal prosecution and civil claims for damage.

A CIP catalogue record for this title is available from the British Library.

ISBN: 978-1-80074-175-1

Everything here is based on truth, but it may not be entirely factual. I have occasionally embroidered. The events are portrayed to the best of the author's memory.

First Published in 2024

Olympia Publishers
Tallis House
2 Tallis Street
London
EC4Y 0AB

Printed in Great Britain

Acknowledgements

This book has been some time in the making and has dealt with some sensitive material. I would like to thank those who recognised the sincerity of its intent and provided support and worthwhile feedback. First and foremost, I would like to thank my family, in particular my remarkable wife, Fiona, for her patience and support and my mother and sister for helping with interviews, finding documents and providing editing and feedback.

My special thanks also to the office of the Commissioner for Children and Young People here in Perth for their content and the concern they offer the children of this state.

Last but not least my thanks to the team at Olympia Publishing for their expertise in producing a top-quality product and belief in myself and the text.

As you read my story I hope it gives you the strength writing it gave me.

Preface

Dr Robinson's summary of my condition in a letter to Dr Staer after I had been in Stubbs Terrace Hospital for two weeks was dated March 25, 1975. It read as follows:

Dear Dr Staer,
    Thank you for referring Paul to this hospital. He was seen by Dr Baxter, who referred him to me.
    Paul was hag ridden by obsessive, compulsive features, complaining that he had to count the number of steps he took and walk in certain ways to avoid overwhelming feelings of anxiety. He has not been attending school; instead of which, he has stayed home, playing by himself, or watching T.V. The interview was repeatedly punctuated by his saying, "Mum can tell you that." He was sleeping badly, frequently waking up and worrying.
    Mrs Kain was a very solicitous woman whose anxiety about Paul was partly conveyed to her husband.
    In view of the disturbing nature of Paul's compulsive obsessive state and his inability to attend school, I admitted him to Stubbs Terrace Hospital.
    He is now attending the local state school (Graylands). His compulsive, obsessive features are less prominent, but I anticipate that he will require to be here for at least for the rest of this term.
    Yours sincerely,
    Dr Robinson (Psychiatrist)

Background

Obsessive-compulsive disorder (OCD) is a mental disorder where people feel the need to check things repeatedly, have certain thoughts repeatedly and feel they need to perform certain routines repeatedly. People are unable to control either the thoughts or actions. (Wikipedia)

Dr Frankenstein's promise if you will be his friend:

> Night time sharpens, heightens each sensation
> Darkness stirs and wakes imagination
> Silently the senses abandon their defences
> Slowly, gently, night unfurls its splendour
> Grasp it, sense it, tremulous and tender
> Turn your face away from the garish light of day
> Turn your thoughts away from cold unfeeling light
> And listen to the music of the night
>
> Close your eyes and surrender to your darkest dreams
> Purge your thoughts of the life you knew before
> Close your eyes, let your spirit start to soar
> And you'll live as you've never lived before
> Softly, deftly, music shall caress you
> Hear it, feel it secretly possess you
> Open up your mind, let your fantasies unwind
> In this darkness that you know you cannot find

> The darkness of the music of the night
> Let your mind start to journey through a strange new world
> Leave all thoughts of the life you knew before
> Let your soul take you where you long to be
> Only then can you belong to me
> Floating, falling, sweet intoxication
> Touch me, trust me savour each sensation
> Let the dream begin, let your darker side give in
> To the power of the music that I write
> The power of the music of the night
> You alone can make my song take flight
> Help me make the music of the night
>
> *The Music of the Night* by Andrew Lloyd Webber

I often played with Dr Frankenstein through the sultry February and March days of 1975 in the Great Southern of Western Australia. He had offered to reshape me for the better. I remember watching *Some Mother's Do 'Ave 'Em* starring the emerging Andrew Lloyd Webber actor Michael Crawford and then finding peace in an evening drive with the family. I took solace from his tortures by looking at the stars and the lights.

Introduction

When I entered the sterile and life-sapping hospital for the first time, all I was thinking about was brightening my day by watching the colour television and leaving early. However, once I stepped through the security threshold, my credibility as a narrator would forever be thrown into question. It now occurs to me that it is unusual for a victim to write a book about their own disorder rather than be observed. Being a narrator is a powerful thing. Perhaps I will lie about the number of obsessive repetitions, the desperation and then the harrowing return to stark reality after the flood of elation. I could also lie about how long it took to clean my teeth, or my mother to clean her teeth for me. Should I explore the effect on people? Perhaps I will ignore the pressure of circumstance that led to such a situation. I hope I have moved on. I hope people believe I have moved on, otherwise I could not write it.

Do I pretend that I was really in control? I was very much not in control. How do I look back in a sane state of mind and justify personal destruction and self-harm? This is not a nice story or epic reflection on life, nor is it an adventure. It is a journey I suppose. Perhaps I have written a book that is best to be read in secret, not shared, and allow an audience to indulge the hope that it is possible to coexist with your deepest fears. I hope to explain with honesty about this monster that sought to take my hopes and dreams and take me to a place I could never come back from. It found the part of me that was indestructible.

Let me describe the monster: in my mind it is like a dark spider, but with talons and many legs, that blots out the sun. It is always night in the monster's world. It has long ram-like horns next to its saliva filled mouth and protruding tusks. Its many eyes seem to command an army of smaller spider minions. It attaches itself like a parasite and grows like a cancer with an endless web that stretches all through your consciousness. It may appear when you are unwary or in the furthermost reaches of your mind, and therefore the minds and lives of the ones you love. It never sleeps, it never eats, it is relentless; it does not know pity or pain. It is driven by only what it has to do. You are helpless in its power. It exposes your frailties, your sensitivities, and your reputation. It has a gun to your head, unseen by all except yourself.

You can never hide from it. At the time it would search and always find me cowering, praying, helpless in its grip and frantic about the effect it might have on myself and others. It could penetrate walls and distance in an instant. You are never safe as it backs you into a corner. Families and communities would be tested. I would lie on the couch offering rosaries in meditation and repetition, but it would toy with my faith. It would throw me off the cliff. I would desperately search for a foothold on the sheer face, but falling further and further, would slide down, until reaching the bottom, crushed, I would see the stars and the moon, and it would be angry with me. As the dust settled, I would be alone with the fiend, and be told by my parents that "it doesn't really matter."

That is the reason for my actions, but I know I will be exploring questions about why a ten-year-old from the country was institutionalised for six months in the city and why he was left, bewildered, to cry his lungs out in an alien environment. If psychiatry was an instrument of social purification, then I was well and truly cured. Perhaps I needed to learn to everyone's satisfaction, especially my parents, about the moral code of society, whatever that is perceived to be. I drew no comfort from knowing that my final mental state was a particularly sanitised one. To me it was overkill. There were no group counselling sessions, no one-on-ones, no outpatient clinics, or occasional visits to the city – just the final solution of being shut away as if one size fitted all and stigma should be imposed. I was powerless against those who have power. How could someone who is happy understand someone who is not? I will be looking for honest answers that won't be swept under the carpet.

This was 1975, in the Great Southern of Western Australia during the state's longest dry spell. It was the year of the Whitlam dismissal and atomic testing in the Pacific Ocean. I remember hearing the song, *Fox on the Run* and *January* by *Pilot*. Pope Paul VI was in office in Rome. At the movies, it was the year of *The Towering Inferno*, *Airport '75* and… *Young Frankenstein*.

Prologue: February 1975

His mother regretted she had not seen it coming. After all he had always been the difficult one. She had nicknamed him "The Ugly Duckling." As an infant he had cried incessantly and would not be placated, changing the family dynamic with his insatiable hunger for attention and the breast. She had been defeated then and now she was simply too busy with the new little ones. There was not enough time to attend to all their needs. She had been forced to make agonising choices with her children, choices that had been made long ago. Now she was sorry she had ignored the talk from her older children that Paul wasn't mixing or was doing strange things in lonely parts of the school by himself. If only her husband hadn't been so sure everything was okay and put it down to "just being a boy."

Now the late afternoon sun beat down on the Great Southern farm. The same as it had yesterday and the same as it would tomorrow. The same as it had done for a record number of rainless days. The leaves were withering and dying in late summer, exhausted and lifeless as they fell off trees. Farmers worshipped the rain. For the crops and stock it was the sustenance of life. The farming family was broken-hearted. Without life-giving water their souls were arid.

In the February dusk a lone child was feeding the chooks, the dogs and the cows. The kelpies would look at him with wide-eyed longing. His homework waited, but the sun went down. His spirit was a patchworked dry dam. His body was performing repetitions to comfort himself in the half-light. Beads of perspiration dotted his forehead, but he would not be comforted. "One, two, three, four, five, six, seven, eight, nine…" he breathlessly whispered to himself. Each repetition making him feel better, but somehow worse. Each was to be the last, until it was found unsatisfying. If only he could tear himself away to the important tasks. He was burdened to perform repetitions, to count the grains, to tie that shoelace again and again and walk that way repeatedly. The dogs barked. They would need feeding again tomorrow and the eggs would need collecting in the morning before school.

Anger and frustration gnawed at him. He knew where he wanted to be. He knew what he wanted to do. He wanted to be important. He wanted to be useful. He wanted to be *The Catcher in the Rye*, but he could not save himself, let alone others. Frustration welled inside him. He would beat it. He would go.
He stayed.
His anger grew to desperation. Did he want this? Did he have a choice? What was normal? Did he need to do this? He should not be here, but he didn't have a choice. The choice was the monster's.

The sun had set. He was alone in the stillness of the dusk and the silhouettes of the moving animals. He fled, head down, watching his flying feet carry him the fifty metres to the safety of the laundry and the light of the outhouse. Breathing heavily, he could make out the first star of the night and made a silent wish for personal peace. He rushed desperately to wash his hands. Again and again he thrust them under the water as the life-giving fluid flowed soothingly from the tap. He thought for a moment he heard a comforting voice from inside the house and continued his lonely vigil.

The Return: Home 1 (August 1975)

Invictus

Out of the night that covers me,
Black as the Pit from pole to pole,
I thank whatever gods may be
For my unconquerable soul.

In the fell clutch of circumstance
I have not winced nor cried aloud.
Under the bludgeoning's of chance
My head is bloody, but unbowed.

Beyond this place of wrath and tears
Looms but the Horror of the shade,
And yet the menace of the years
Finds, and shall find, me unafraid.

It matters not how strait the gate,
How charged with punishments the scroll.
I am the master of my fate:
I am the captain of my soul.

William Ernest Hemley

In later years I would reflect back on William Ernest Hemley's poem and think how apt it was for my return to the family and town. I perceived that my coming back to Narrogin was "the horror of the shade" and for the community the scroll of my punishments was long. I did know for a fact that my greatest gift was "my unconquerable soul."

I drove home from the mental institution with my father in relative silence. It was the seventies and the family's white Holden Kingswood was an iconic choice. Appearances were everything in the seventies, especially the representation of the "happy family." To me it was what was underneath that was more important. Cyclone Tracey had just blown through Darwin and the dismissal of the Whitlam government would happen later that year.

The road snaked innocently through the meandering hills and pine plantations in Western Australia's Great Southern from Perth to Narrogin, as if it could not know of the burial ground for murder victims that it would become. It was a road I had travelled very often in the previous few months. My father had the need for speed. As the trees flashed past at one hundred and forty kilometres an hour he was left to his thoughts and me to mine. I don't suppose there was much for a farmer to talk about with their ten-year-old son, given the circumstances. I didn't think he would want to talk about the diabetics, obsessive compulsives, broken homes and children with suicidal tendencies. Although my father loved me, for him it was many bridges too far. Perhaps he didn't think a ten-year-old should be subject to those issues, and certainly not his son.

Dad was an Irish Catholic and the father of five children. He was nicknamed "The Pope" by his farming neighbours for his overt devotion to Catholicism: he was Chairman of the local Catholic school board, and like the pontiff, quite bald. To his family and friends, his first name, Eugene, became Hugh, Hughie, Ewie, or to his nieces and nephews, Uncle Ew. He once told me that his name was his cross to bear. He was a charming man and leader in his own way. He spoke and expressed opinions clearly, but struggled with the written word and did not communicate feelings well. His family were stalwarts of the local footy club. With his brothers he had played in a series of premierships. He was very much one of the boys. Perhaps he was best known for being a producer of fine grade wool and successful businessman, even though his property was not particularly big. He regularly had one of the best prices in the district. His children were reminded to never reveal what it was. I idolised his masculinity and often wished that he cared for me as much as his sheep. To his family he was defined by his masculinity. A shearer and horseman, he lived the dream of being the "man's man;" he could drink hard and his V8 car was valued. He was strongly built, but not tall, and in today's vernacular he may have been "punching above his weight," especially as time passed him by. He had a claim on being the alpha male of his clan, but it would be hotly contested, not least of all, ironically, by his sons.

I always desperately wanted Dad to be proud of me, his baby-faced blonde curly haired boy, rather than hide me somewhere. Two years earlier I thought I had achieved this when I won Junior Boy Champion at the interschool athletics carnival in Narrogin. This was a good achievement as our Catholic school was tiny and we would compete, with a handicap, against much larger, government, schools. I was quite a celebrity for a short while as

I was paraded before my peers at assembly. The monster was nowhere to be seen.

It had been hard work in the time leading up to the carnival. I would get out of bed early and practice so I could grasp the chance to be the apple of my father's eye. It was worth the bleeding feet and facing the freezing and often frosty Great Southern early spring mornings. I would sneak out of bed at the crack of dawn and tiptoe past my younger siblings to practice before school. Sometimes, they would stir and ask me where I was going. I would simply reply that I was off to make sure I won at the interschools. Dad had even given me some advice: "Never look sideways and keep your eyes on the finishing tape."

    I would practice this over and over again by going into my crouch and shouting "Bang!" I had no formal training, but my long legs would fly like pistons down the seventy metre track that I had paced out on the most even part of the house paddock that I could find. It became well-worn as soft divots were dislodged. In my imagination I could hear the crowd cheering as I neared the end of the race. I had to get faster and faster. Take longer strides. Watch the tape. Fight back. The crowd reached a crescendo as I neared the end of the track. I breasted the imaginary tape and threw my arms high in exaltation. I looked around and a Hereford cow was chewing its cud, hardly impressed.

In the same way, I couldn't wait for the afternoons and would push to get home. I longed for when my feet would once again fly down the homemade track past the barley grass and the animal dung with only the bovines for company and the occasional moo for conversation. Sometimes, I would combine running with getting the cows in for my father to milk the following morning, before returning to the house for tea.

I didn't know a lot about the opposition, but I was aware that I was good at, and enjoyed running. I had gone through a growth spurt and knew that anything could happen on the day. It was more than just sprinting, of course: there was also the flag race and jumps. I loved being at the carnival that meeting. The grass was so green, and the track was fast. There were no livestock or hills, just the fresh scent of newly cut grass, cheering spectators, colour and action. In fact, it was much as I imagined it in my practice. I started out with high aspirations. I won my championship sprint. I was good over the first forty and felt like I was taking off at the start of the race. After that I knew that I would be hard to beat for the trophy. I certainly got it right in the triple jump. I remember the judge saying after my final leap: "That will probably do it for you." It certainly did. It was a record that stood for thirty years. It was a special day, a day of fantasy where I lived what I played out in the paddocks. The opposition simply fell away. The images at the carnival mingled with the ones in my imagination at practice and fed on each other. The crowd were hushed at the start and cheering my name at the end.

My family were there. I heard my father call near the end of a race, "Come on, Paul, you can do it!" People respected and looked up to me. I was "it." There was a stirring at the meet. Could this lad be the Junior Champion Boy representing St Matthews?

At the end of the carnival I sat down with the other competitors, taking my place among the red-shirted juniors at St Matt's. As I waited for the trophy presentations, I felt satisfied that the day had gone well. I still couldn't believe it when my name was called out as the winner. Not green, not gold, but red. The announcer called out the runner-up Junior Boy first and I thought to myself *I beat that dude* and my heart rate quickened. He continued, "...and the Junior Boy champion, representing St Matthews... Paul Kain." I nearly toppled over. I had done it. The training and early mornings had been worth it. I found my dad's face among the spectators. He was beaming and taking a few handshakes. I was rapturous. The most important thing was that I had my father's acceptance at last.

A principal presented the trophy and the spectators wanted to hear from me. What could I say? I heard the St Matt's crowd yelling "Speech! Speech!" I had to say something for them.

"Thanks," I eventually mumbled into the large squarish microphone they put in front of my face and hoped that covered it. My first public speaking attempt had not been a success, but I hoped they would forgive me.

Years later at the same carnival, but in Year 7, I would wonder about how easy I had found it and how things had fallen into place on that special day. My growth spurt had well and truly stopped, my peers had caught up and the prestige of winning had been lost. I no longer competed in the championship events and was relegated to the lowly age race. At least I thought I would win that. I began badly and was behind all the way. I was waiting to catch up, but never did. My red singlet finished behind a sea of green and yellow and I wasn't even on the podium. In fact, I was insultingly beaten by a familiar opponent from my own school. He rubbed salt into the wounds by insisting I was crying after the race. Maybe I was. I was back to square one in my quest for my father's acceptance.

"Are you over it then?" Dad asked casually as we raced through the Roleystone foothills. He was smoking, as he often did in the days before it became unfashionable, and ash flickered over his lime green safari suit.

"Over what?" I replied innocently. I noticed my father used a tone that insinuated I had just gotten over the flu and might still be contagious. I spoke through thin and strained lips. My skin was pulled taut over my facial features, from my wide mouth to my clear forehead. Vaguely, I remembered that people with thin lips were supposed to be mean-spirited and even cruel. By contrast, I had also read somewhere that lips became thin and tight from years of pain. I wondered which the reason was for mine. Perhaps, I concluded, they were just inherited. In any case, I knew that worrying about it could not change the size of your lips.

"You know... the monster. Have you beaten him?" Dad pulled his eyes off the road to glance at me blankly and took a draw on his Winfield.

I thought of the popular and well-known Winfield advertising slogan with Paul Hogan starring in his sleeveless flannelette shirt. "Anyhow, have a Winfield," he would say.

"Of course I've beaten the monster," I replied. Deep inside I felt the ache where his talons had scratched and the healed over wounds were still tender. I added the confession, "I had to betray you though."

Dad responded with a reference to the New Testament. "I suppose it's like when Jesus was fasting in the desert. Satan took him to the highest peak and promised him all he could see if he bowed down and worshipped him, and Jesus refused."

"Jesus was too smart for that."

"You were too smart too. That was your trouble. You

overcame things and now it's like General MacArthur and his return to the Philippines." I laughed inwardly at his gross hyperbole.

"I thought I was a corporal, not a general."

"I'm sorry," Dad hesitated. "What do you mean?"

"You know, 'Corpy,' my nickname. Uncle John and you always call me 'Corpy'. You know, like Lance-Corporal Albert Jacka, the first Victoria Cross winner for Australia." Dad laughed at that.

"I actually want to be more than a corporal," I said.

"Why's that?"

"So then I can use nuclear bombs on people. You know, like they do in the Pacific. The other nickname you gave me was 'Pea Bea.' I guess after the fly spray. It seems to have caught on."

Dad seemed to choke on his cigarette and took a moment to recover himself. "Anyway," he said after he had got his breath back. "Have a Whitlam and Gough yourself to death." His politics were always right wing and he laughed at the common play on the Winfield ad.

He had been an active campaigner for the pro-catholic DLP at that time in the seventies. He hated Gough Whitlam with a passion. The car had often been filled with yellow DLP pamphlets as he drove the streets of Narrogin and then carried them with fellow supporters to door knock. He had been among those to heckle when that Prime Minister had come to Perth just before his dismissal, in his white suit, to address a rally of farmers and left with it covered in stains from rotten tomatoes. It could be guessed that Whitlam had known what was coming that morning when he dressed and wanted to highlight what arrogant savages the farmers of the Western Australian Wheatbelt were.

"Maybe we should just stick with Paul," he said eventually. Dad loved his nicknames. This was alluded to in the eulogy at his funeral years later. It was said that even a few days after entering the pearly gates he would have a nickname for the Virgin Mary.

Dad became more amiable as the road fell away to gravel and we could see his farmland and that of the neighbours. We turned down the mile-long driveway at the farm sign: "Cooramining: E.F. Kain." It made me proud of my dad, but left little doubt that you were entering his domain. I thought the sign was unfair as he didn't actually live there by himself, but it was typical of the times and similar to many other farm signs in the district.

Dad had purchased the farm in about 1955 and the house was the original one. It was a scenic, rolling property and the homestead was the centrepiece where the family had grown up. An aerial photo from the early 1960s featured bush and tree clumps rushing to conceal the network of tracks and roads around the house. It created the impression of a small hamlet or grain siding town, with arms extending to the series of sheds, silos, machinery and small animal yards. Longer fences indicated the end of the homestead and the start of the pastoral land with the dotting of stock. An early longing of mine involved the desire to climb those fences and explore the world beyond. More than once, as a toddler, I commenced my quest, only to have a bloody encounter with the cruel barbed strand along the top of the perimeter and then have to race back inside to tell my distraught mother that the fence had "stung me."

My first memories of the house itself were happy ones and there were many photographs of my father with Simon and I. If the photos are to be believed, in the time before the arrival of my three other siblings, I was bought up being driven around in wheelbarrows, feeding lambs and holding hands with my older brother. Dad appeared to enjoy being a young father. I certainly remember waking to the bleating of sheep and the tramp of boots on the veranda as he arrived back from milking with a full bucket of frothing warm milk, and more often than not, some eggs from the chicken coop or vegetables from the garden. The house became my world and an entity of self-sufficiency and discovery. I would follow my dad around when I could, as he cut wood, fixed machinery and tended sheep. Evenings would be spent playing with my brother on the floor of the farmhouse as we wondered about and listened to the world outside, before we were prayed for and taken to our shared bedroom to be settled for the night. I was not encouraged in my early efforts to venture. I was late starting school and attended hardly any kindergarten. It was as if nothing else was needed.

I was awakened from my reflections of the house by the Kingswood disturbing the loose gravel as it pulled into the main driveway. The roar of its V8 engine was audible from some distance and the family would certainly have seen us coming down the entrance road. My mother must have sighed and thought *I hope no one mentions the words "loony bin,"* but I stepped out of the station wagon to the stillness of the spring afternoon. My family was lined up and waiting. There was my older brother, Simon, my younger sister, Jenny, and younger brothers, Nick and Daniel. No one ran at me with pitchforks or shotguns. What was I really expecting? I had been home for weekends, but this time I was here to stay. I certainly felt like an outsider, but perhaps it was just me. I knew I would be brought back to earth when people looked at me strangely.

Mum rushed to give me a hug and welcome back her ten-year-old adventurer, dressed in his favourite jeans and blue and white anorak. "Welcome home, darling," she said as my unkempt blonde hair bobbled with the force. I vaguely remember wondering if I had washed it recently. I knew that chewing my nails was a problem and a bad habit.

"I'm back," I managed to utter, making an effort not to chew my nails. "Did you miss me? Have I changed? I must have grown at least."

"Yes, things are different now," Simon replied. He still had his helmet on. I noticed the 100cc ag motorbike parked on the grass. I was pleased that he was acknowledging that the situation of my going away was hard to understand and gave him a high five.

"Of course, we all missed you, darling," Mum cut in through quivering lips. "It's so wonderful to have you back for good. The family is together again." The farm's setting was the same way I remember it, but things were somehow different. The weight of the world wasn't pushing in.

"So, what was it like?" Jenny asked me, cutting to the chase as usual. She was two years younger than me, almost to the day, and always interested in adventures in the outside world. She would later confide, however, that sometimes she found my behaviour frightening.

What was it like? How can I begin to tell? "Well, the hospital part started in Dr Robinson's office," I responded.

Tough Love: Away 1 (March 1975)

Was that a toy Dalek from the *Doctor Who* TV series that I saw on Dr Robinson's desk? Well, it was 1975 and *Dr Who* was all the rage. It must have even amused the bored child psychiatrist who had everything. I pushed a button; a series of half-submerged lights came on in the toy's lower half and a plunger moved in and out. "Exterminate! Exterminate! You are an enemy of the Daleks," it vibrated in its mechanised robotic voice. The switch was turned to green and Dr Robinson must have been playing with it.

"Yes, Cowan, he's here now, the country boy. The worst thing you can do is show him sympathy." He was oblivious to me as he continued on the phone.

"Exterminate!" The shrill, robotic voice seemed to get more guttural, slower and sound out the syllables. "Ex... term... in... ate!" I couldn't believe that a grown man was playing with a Dalek toy and wondered if he might be in more need of help than I was. Maybe he needed it to ease the pain for all concerned.

"There are four other siblings... what's our quota for funding situation?" He paused to listen to the reply. "*Hmm*, well how long does he have to stay...? That long, really...! No, well, we've never had anyone for that long." He seemed to drag out the last two words. I thought actually that he looked a bit like Davros, the creator of the Daleks. He was incredibly old, and I believed he could have done with a mobile control unit to whiz around on. He might once have been handsome, but I seriously doubted it. He wore square, thick-rimmed glasses and his grey hair was too long at the front and fell down the back of his neck in long curls. His crisp white shirt had just discernible coffee stains on one cuff. He continued talking on the phone. "Yes, I know Williams is officially in charge, but you're my man on the inside. I've got better things to do… he should be over soon anyway."

As he finished the call, my attention was drawn to some strange paintings on the walls. It was hard to tell what they were of, but they seemed to contain the human form. I thought my art teacher at school could have done better. It was almost as if Dr Robinson had done them himself. Perhaps he had.

Like an enemy before Davros, I was utterly powerless as the psychiatrist stared at me from behind his large oaken desk. A brilliant man, but like Davros he was to show no pity. Even an adult would surely have been intimidated by having their sanity questioned and stripped to the bone. I was in a child-sized chair at the end of his table, a writhing and distressed ten-year-old country boy at the mercy of the professional academic. He seemed to me to be very tall. I kept staring at his impressive white moustache. Was it a symbol of his standing? I considered for a moment that I ought to be on my best behaviour as I was all dressed up – new tartan trousers and formal shirt – but why was I seeing him by myself and not with my parents? I didn't realise at the time that he had my fate in his hands, or perhaps he was the rubber stamp that my parents wanted. I decided that he was just another doctor, and it was just another day, but I was to be proven so wrong. I imagined him with a Mohawk haircut and googly eyes. In my mind's eye, the monster's talons were reaching out for him, the slobbering jaw was dripping on his blue tie. *How would he feel about that,* I thought? *Where would he run screaming? How would he comfort himself?* He finally seemed to notice me.

"Well, let's begin with a head measurement," he said. *Are you for real*, I thought? *What's that got to do with anything?* As an adult looking back, I realised the pointlessness of this outdated diagnostic tool. He took out some elaborate apparatus and began measuring my cranium. "How old are you, Paul?"

"Ten," I replied. I wondered how I had gotten myself into this situation. Here I was at Princess Margaret Hospital for Children in Perth, alone in a large office behind an enormous double door with a respected psychiatrist measuring my head to assess my sanity.

It was to be the last day of my cavalier attitude towards the medical profession. I would never forget my lesson. If I had known that he had the authority to recommend electric shock therapy or permanently mind-altering drugs, I would not have entered his office maddened, irrational and crying. I was trying to affect my parents, not the doctor. Whether he was very good at his job or not was not the point to me? In any case, to him I was displaying all the symptoms. I needed my parents. They would put things right. Dad was here. That had to be good.

"Tell me what the problem is, Paul," he implored, looking across from the other side of his wide desk. I just continued sobbing. I would never tell him. It was my only bargaining chip. He persisted, even offering a smile that showed off his gold fillings and overwhelming halitosis. "I can't help you if you won't talk to me. Your parents have journeyed a long way and my time is limited." He looked frustrated and actually grabbed my arm with force. "You must tell me. I know what your problem is." The thought passed through my mind that if he knew what the problem was, why did I have to tell him?

"The spider." I managed through my fear to speak at last.

"A spider... where?" He looked around in alarm.
"In me... a monster."
"I'm sorry, I don't follow." He was silent for a time. "You must tell me, Paul, or I can't help you."
"The... monster..."
"Yes... the monster... go on."
"I am... the... monster," I blurted out loudly. So now he had it. He knew my secret. He had won. I l looked at him in anger and he looked at me, both dumbfounded and in triumph.
"Mum will tell you more," I sobbed. Did he seriously expect me to tell him about the bully, about endless repetitions or about spending evenings in self-imposed repetitive prayer?
"Is there something we can work together on here?" He seemed to be staring down at my crying form.
"If there is, Mum will know," I replied.
He again looked distressed, but continued on. "How are things going at school?" Perhaps I only had myself to blame that the appointment did not go well. I certainly did not tell him what he wanted to hear. In retrospect, in this type of situation, if you do not tell people what they want to hear you may be subject to the consequences. It must have been all I was capable of at the time. "I have a little hospital," he said at last. "I was just speaking to a psychiatric nurse there. It's live in, but it might help sort out this monster business."

I kept on crying. I thought the sadder I was the more unlikely my treatment would be severe. I certainly didn't consider for a moment that I would be left in Perth with strange people at my time of need straight after the appointment. Mum and Dad were with Dr Robinson for a long time while I sat in the waiting room and sobbed. They came out flustered, and I thought, in conspiracy. I felt a little comfort that at least they were back. We could go home now. Our expedition was over. I mopped away a few tears. A few minutes later I learnt my fate had been decided. I felt powerless. What could I do?

"We have some news for you, Paul," Mum announced. "Doctor Robinson said he had a hospital in the city that will help you and you will like. You can come and see us on weekends after a few weeks. He says it's for the best. It might even be exciting, an adventure." I felt amazed that my mother had already decided that I would like it.

As my father drove to my new home, I had my nose fixed closely to the window. It was a hot and humid March Day. Perth, it seemed, was even hotter than Narrogin. My sweaty fingers left greasy streaks on the glass. How was I to stay if I had no clothes or personal items? As we drove in I noticed the black boys. They were everywhere and quite fascinating with their mixture of charcoal and sprouting shoots. The hospital backed onto bushland and was beautiful and green with lush gardens. It was next to Lemnos Hospital and close to Grayland's institution. It was in the same area, but did not have the same sense of officialdom, as if it had been added on as an afterthought. It appeared to be like a normal, if oversized house, with red brick squares and columns jutting out at various angles into nowhere in particular. It had no protective fence or patients in white gowns and was full of young people, or so I was told. I wondered why it was so big for a building that was built like a house and what secrets were imprisoned behind the walls. I was soon to find out.

The Monster: Home 2 (Summer 1969)

My earliest vivid memory of the farm was the day I made a pact with the monster when I was just five. Dad used to cart water to the house from a standpipe using a car-sized metal tank covered with black tar that took two men to roll into position. There was no fibreglass in those days. It was placed on a tall and long flatbed trailer hooked by a pin to the old blue tractor. The Fordson was an icon of farming in Australia in the sixties. I remember when Dad wasn't looking, I would sit up high on the worn metal seat, stare around the vertical exhaust and play with the steering wheel. I wanted to be like my father and even though I felt dwarfed by the equipment around me, my young self was driven by my pride in it. I could not see the danger.

As he was driving I would cling to the mesh grille on the front of the trailer and smile at my dad whenever he turned around to check on me. I saw him bouncing on the seat as the trailer and tank pitched up and down as it hit the holes and ridges in the paddocks. I thought I was safe. I was with Dad. It didn't occur to me that the full tank was secured only by a wooden railway sleeper on each side. It was always an adventure, but on this day things got out of hand.

It was a clear and hot February morning. The paddocks were dry and the stubbles hard and yellow after the harvest. To me it was a world of snakes, red backs and kangaroos. I saw the snakes and red backs in my sleep. My time was spent avoiding insects, mostly huntsman spiders. They were enormous hairy brutes. I imagined them with teeth and pincers, but I was brave as I had the insulation of my father. This day I was so confident I wore no shoes, only shorts and a T-shirt. I felt the wind rushing through my blonde, curly locks. I was jolting with the bumps as we climbed a grassy hilltop. Visible at the base of the hilltop was the mast of the red windmill. As we got closer its size increased, but its age and brokenness became apparent. Its once bright paint had faded and its former mighty sails had collapsed meekly like wilted petals on the main frame. Disconnected long ago, it remained a loyal guardian of a different era. Recently, I had played with Simon among the white gums around its base. Red ant nests inhabited the sandy white soil. Urging each other on we poked them with sticks and watched them scurry heroically from their holes to confront the intruders, before we panicked as their numbers overwhelmed us. "Ants! Ants!" My brother would scream as stinging welts appeared on our small bare feet and we would run crying to Dad at his work filling the tank.

"Dad, help," I chimed in, desperate for attention and hoping he could ease the pain. "The ants are eating me."

"No, they wouldn't do that," he replied laconically and with sardonic humour. "Those red ants are pretty fussy about what they eat." My father was a disciplinarian and must have figured that we shouldn't have been playing with ants in the first place.

My mind returned to being on top of the hill and enjoying my ride. I looked down over the wire grille and was fascinated by the link pin jumping up and down. The yellow barely grass was long. You could not see the little gullies and dips. At the time I did not consider it dangerous that I was riding on a trailer on bumpy

ground connected only to the tractor by an uncovered draw pin. Up went the pin then back in the slot, once, twice, then I was in the air as if in slow motion. The front of the trailer had gouged into the soil and for me it was like hitting an invisible force field. My foot slipped on the metal tray and my fingers lost their grip. I clutched at handfuls of air as I groped for a hold.
I was falling.
I was going to die.
My world turned to grey mist. For a fleeting instant, I wondered why there was no sun. The tractor was gone. Dad was gone. I was only a rag doll against the trailer and the full tank. I was thrown violently in the air. Time stood still. A desperate voice inside me said, "Hold on to life! Don't give up."

I don't remember knocking my ankle on the trailer as I fell, only that I couldn't move afterwards. I landed perfectly, but painfully, on my behind. Looking up, I saw the full tank wobbling, finding resistance only from the sole wooden sleeper that kept it from falling down the now angled trailer. Inch by inch the sleeper began to give way. Fear began creeping into my mind and turned into horror. Emerging out of the mists of my terror and holding back the tank, I saw for the first time the vague outline of the monster. The silhouette stopped almost within touching distance. He seemed to be taking pride in his revelation. As the mists cleared, I saw what must have been a smile through his horribly formed features. I hoped the mist would not clear, but clear it did to reveal the full hideousness of the segmented hide, tough like a rhinoceros and made up of razor sharp diamond shaped segments. The odour burned my nostrils, and in my panic, I believed he was talking to me. "Do you know what the release of this tank will do to you?" He asked. "Death will not be immediate. It will first roll onto your feet and legs, crushing bones as it goes. You will be screaming in agony as your hips are broken and your intestines are minced. Every lower joint will be dislocated and muscles stretched out of position. The hard shell will lacerate your skin and by the time the tank gets to your heart you will be beyond recognition. Your father will not recognise your bloody, mangled corpse. All your hopes and dreams will be lost… gone forever."

His razor talons stopped the tank. As he did he branded his deal deep inside my subconscious. His promise was simple: "Be mine and live." I chose life. The tank teetered over the sleeper for a long second and fell back on the trailer. The talons changed to the tank's tar covering, the eyes turned to droplets and splashes and the sun returned.

Dad found me there a few minutes later, still looking up at the tank. He had raced back, leaving the tractor to crash into a tree. He would spend days fixing it. He scooped me up in his arms and we began to walk home. "Are you all right?" he asked. "Oh, Pauly, I'm sorry, so sorry."

"A disfrin, a disfrin, I need a disfrin!" I managed to gasp. I thought a headache pill that I often saw my parents take would make everything better.

"We'll get you a disprin when we get home," he replied quietly, but assuredly.

The Kid Master: Away 2 (March 1975)

At the hospital Mum and Dad introduced me to my assigned psychiatric nurse, Gordon Peers, the "Kid Master." Like my father I used nicknames and his became "GP," which he didn't seem to mind. He was to become my dad for the six months I was to be there. In later years I would reflect on him as like the character of O'Brien from the novel *1984*, my torturer and friend. I would think, meeting him for the first time was like being anaesthetised, you felt good when it happened, but the pain would kick in later. He had arrived punctually at the hospital. He got off his powerful motorcycle, that I was immediately envious of, and struck me as an imposing figure. In his mid-thirties, he was not particularly tall, but he had a lush red beard and freckled skin. To me he seemed red and hairy like a huntsman spider. He wore jeans, black leathers and gloves. His helmet was emblazoned with the Australian flag. He had a commanding presence, but the demeanour of a man who was used to other people doing his bidding because they liked him. His eyes were soft and kindly, but the lines in his face were severe and I knew I wouldn't like him to give me "the look."

"Hey, Boss," he said in the manner of someone who was used to being in complete control, "it looks like you and I are going to be in partnership."

"Are we going to be friends?" I asked.

"You bet, Paul," came the confident reply, "but lighten up, you look like you're in pain." He then addressed my parents. "Hi,

I'm Gordon Peers. You must be Mr and Mrs Kain," he said in a charming manner. I thought his eyes lingered on my mother for a moment too long. "Welcome, I'm Paul's assigned nurse. We just have to fix up some paperwork." We walked with him for the first time through the automatic doors into the foyer containing reception desk and offices. It smelt strongly of new carpet and air freshener. The adults disappeared into the office. It seems I was to be processed and rubber stamped.

GP returned by himself reasonably promptly and explained that my parents had gone to buy some clothes for me and would be back soon. He passed over some odd looking pills and some water. "This should help things," he said. "Nothing like getting some merchandise into you."

"Are they disprin?" I asked naively.

"Actually, something a bit stronger. It will help when your parents leave." I thought I caught him smirking. "You've done your dash. We own your little white arse now your parents have signed you up. You take what we give you so come and meet the gang." His tone had changed after my parents left. I felt like I had been chewed up and spat out.

I followed GP meekly through to the living area. We had to pass through the double security doors of the checkpoint. It was a barrier into a world where I expected I would be completely insignificant. *No going back now,* I thought. I made myself feel better by thinking perhaps they might have a colour television, but was to be disappointed even on that score. We walked into a hallway and entered a large living area or rumpus room with a black and white TV, beanbags and two smaller rooms, with toys in them, at the rear. It looked like fun. Suddenly, an older boy appeared from nowhere and almost knocked me over with his extended horizontal arms as, he literally, flew past. "Clear the way," he cried. "I'm on a plane to Poofter's Paradise." *Yep, no arguments here mate*, I thought.

"That's just Rennie," a younger girl called. "He's angry because he hasn't got any friends."

Rennie stopped and stared at me. I noticed his sharpened ears and impish sneer. "He looks like a crier to me," he said abruptly and then spoke to nobody in particular. "Do I have any takers on this dude being a crier?"

"Yeah, he could be, Rennie. He looks a bit soft," replied a male patient walking down the corridor.

"Well, just remember to give me something for being right." With that he continued down the long and wide corridor. "Join my plane, join my plane," he pleaded. My first thought was that Dad would not like that guy, but GP didn't seem perturbed. I went back to looking at the large common room with garish orange flowers on the pronounced mantles, matching similar coloured beanbags on the floor. Young patients were strewn around the room in casual poses that matched the décor. Without warning, I felt faint. The room began to spin as the drugs GP had given me kicked in. They definitely had not been disprin. The orange flowers seemed to come off the walls and I had a floating sensation as I tried to ride on them. In reality, I grasped at whatever I could to stop me keeling over and clung to the top of the sofa. *Sesame Street* was on television and Big Bird was reaching his long neck out of the screen and talking to me personally. I felt his soft feathers against my skin. I had experienced awful mind battles with the monster, but I had never felt such nausea as I did now. I felt green. GP looked at me as if he had expected my dizziness.

"Don't worry, Boss. It will pass soon and you'll feel just great," he said. Strangely enough I soon did start to feel happier as I was fussed over, although I knew it was a hollow emotion. He introduced me to a thin older girl named Diane who was picking at her skin, and a good looking fellow about my own age named Bruce who had a series of knife scars on his lower arm. They were dressed in uniforms and had evidently just arrived back from their school day.

"Are you going to the room?" Diane asked in an exaggeratedly sophisticated tone. She smelt of freshly sprayed 4711 cologne.

"I'm sorry, what do you mean?" I had only just walked in. I wasn't aware of any special room and wondered if her comment stemmed from my absent state.

GP interrupted, "And this is Mr Martin." He gestured to a young dark male nurse playing chess with a patient. "He's on staff here."

"Welcome to the gang," he said to me. Then speaking directly to GP, he enquired, "Is that your shockie? At least he's got strides with nice flares." I did not follow what a shockie was. I was beginning not to trust my senses or version of reality. GP soon changed the subject as the afternoon tea trolley arrived along with the prescribed medications.

"Come and get your pills, boys and girls." He said it as if he was handing out Christmas presents. Four or five children appeared in school uniform as GP took on a Pied Piper role. Like dogs with wagging tales, and some giggling, they gathered around the tea trolley. They were pleased to see him.

One greeted him with, "Hi, Gordon, good to see you're early for your shift."

"How's it going? Hey, Gordon's here," called a female

patient.

Another patient who was struggling for attention spoke from the back of the group. "How's your day been, Gordon?" They wanted to touch and hug him as he dished out the food and pills.

"Something for everyone from Uncle Gordon," he laughed. "Nothing more for you though, Paul." I stayed next to Gordon. I thought it was a good place to be.

"It seems you're the boss around here," I observed.

"Well, sort of," he replied. "A friend of mine is a someone in this place."

GP continued to show me around. We went into the dining room and the industrial kitchen. I met a girl a bit older than me who washed a banana and an orange before she peeled and ate them. In a sobering moment I noticed "MHS" branded on many kitchen items. We walked back up the corridor and through a large door that was the gateway to a series of rooms that created a network like rabbit warrens. One had a table tennis table in it, another had a red sign stating officially in block letters: "No Admittance."

"What's in that room?" I asked GP. I felt the spider stir.

"What room?" He seemed uncomfortable that I had even noticed it. I pointed my finger.

"Oh, that room. That's for crazy people."

"Am I crazy?" I asked earnestly. He put his arm around me.

The bedrooms were up a set of mezzanine stairs either side of a hallway that ran through to the rear entrance and the playground. There were single and group rooms, all homely. I was to start in a group room sleeping next to Roy, but would later move into a single. The play area out the back looked good. It had a flying fox that ran out into the native bush, sports courts, and like everything else in the hospital, was extremely big. I told myself I would not be placated as the monster was not happy. It was possibly somewhere I could be my own person.

GP and I walked to the foyer area as my parents returned to check I had settled in and passed on the necessities they had bought for me, including a handsome new watch. *Right, the fun's over*, I thought. *This is an interesting place, but let's go home.* Mum and Dad looked at each other sadly. "You should say your goodbyes," Gordon Peers said.

"We'll be back in a few days, darling," Mum said. "We'll bring you your things and some gifts from home." We moved out the front door and into the car park.

"No," I said. "I'm not being bought off. I'm coming with you." Tears streamed down my face. Mum was crying too and had smudged her make-up, but Dad was stoic in his masculinity and belied his feelings, at least I guessed he did.

"Be brave, my little man," Mum whispered.

Gordon restrained me by holding my midriff, ignoring how his chest was being pummelled by my elbows, and whispered, "Best to stay here, champ. The decision's been made." It was a decision that my mother later said would not be made in this day and age of political correctness. Certainly not for a six-month stint for a country child. No one knew at that stage how long it would be for, or did they? "Come on, Boss. Let's go inside and settle in." My thoughts were *Hey, what are you doing? What's going on here? Is this for real*? It soon became apparent that what I thought was happening WAS actually happening. I pinched myself.

The family car representing my world and aspirations drove slowly out onto the unfamiliar dual carriageway without me.

What about my school? What about my brothers and sisters? I was left in a place that was not my own with a new family and carers that were strangers. I wanted to go to sleep and wake up at home with the sheep bleating and the birds chirping, in my own bed, next to my own family. It was not heaven, but it was better than this. I could not move. I could not speak. Like a zombie I stood stunned. I remember the overcast sky, the cool breeze and the descending dusk. Had an evening ever been this grim? I hoped not and I said a quick prayer of supplication that I would never feel this way again. My parents had left me. The people that I needed most had betrayed me. They said I was a school refuser. Actually, I don't remember refusing school and Mum later admitted it was exaggerated, although I certainly wasn't happy at school.

It was called "tough love," but did it really need to be done? It was definitely unusual. I was a child from a country town, a long way from home. In retrospect it was overkill. I don't think the hospital was designed for this, a halfway house for country ten-year-olds. Perhaps I was an optional extra. I wondered if it had been the easy way out for my parents. Was it the plan all the way along? Whose plan was it? Was it love, or just tough? As the months would pass and I stayed, was that "tougher love?" I was the victim. I was the reality and not the textbook. I was the problem and not a generalisation or statistic. I was Frankenstein's monster, created and then left. Now to endure the pain.

The information and diagnosis in the admission records seemed like Greek to me. It did at the time. It still does. I didn't believe I had a major problem of rudeness and disrespect towards women. I was only ten for heaven's sake. What was I, some version of a pre-pubescent misogynist? I loved my mother, sister and aunties.

As I moved with GP back into the hospital it felt odd, strangely sterile in fact. It certainly was not the smell of home. It contained strange people as carers. The food was different. The hospital had its own social structure and new tiers of responsibility and egotism. It was a completely foreign community that was a shock to the system. I knew I would learn other stories and get to know the staff, but my life would never be the same. I had now seen and learnt about abandonment. There had been too much torment, regret, and to my mind, disloyalty. *What were these people prepared to do?* They didn't know about farms. They didn't know about milking cows or collecting eggs. They didn't know about the amazing sunsets that could be seen from standing on the back fence and looking over the hay shed. They had never felt the comfort of the early evening Albany doctor that came soothingly, wafting the branches of the tall farm gum trees and stirring the topsoil on the dry paddocks. Instead, they knew about early afternoon sea breezes and beaches that went on forever. They knew of green parks and large shopping centres. Little wonder they were different. To me they had done the worst thing they could. They had taken what I perceived as needing the most. I was worried I would die here. I sat on the mezzanine steps and began to cry and scream my heart out.

Horror at Dusk: Home 3 (February 1975)

It had always been the dusk and fear of the unknown that got the better of me. I much preferred some light at night to total darkness. After sunset, stars could be seen clearly, and it was always cooler. The world would slow down, relax, and let the night lights be seen. The beauty of the sparkling refractions of a light show was the reward for surviving the day. If I could see lights, I could self-soothe for a few moments with a reminder that the concrete world was still there and not going anywhere. That light could illuminate what you thought was mundane. There was so much darkness on a farm and my parents didn't ever realise what comfort I could get from an evening drive where there were lights.

Unfortunately, dusk was the worst time. This was the especially the case if Dad had killed a sheep for meat that day and I was caught doing chores near the carcass over at the farm shed. One evening in February 1975, I had commenced my chores while he was still butchering a fat lamb. *Creedence Clearwater Revival* were playing on the local commercial radio:

> I see a bad moon a-rising,
> I see trouble on the way
> I see earthquakes and lightnin'
> I see bad times today

I hope you got your things together
I hope you are quite prepared to die
Looks like we're in for nasty weather
One eye is taken for an eye

Don't go round tonight
It's bound to take your life
There's a bad moon on the rise

The realization that the sun was going down and nothing more could be achieved on the farm for the day caused anxiety. I feared the monster making it difficult for me to finish a day that could never be repeated. It was a time of desperation and black fantasy. Animals in the darkness became moving silhouettes. In my mind, after dusk, their talons would come out and their claws would grow. Chickens would become vengeful. Sometimes in the early evening I would collect the eggs or empty the food scraps in the coop. I would face the daily ritual of their world as they sought to sacrifice themselves on my body by impalement. Each one became a blurring, pecking, clawing projectile. Like me they were blind, desperate, and not discriminating in the darkness. I had watched them during the day seeking out the weak among each other. If they found blood they would pounce on the victim as a group, and peck feathers, flesh and sinew, scratching and tearing until there was only a torn and bleeding carcass. My horror was unimaginable. I would take the scratches and the thuds and listen to the sound of my heavy breaths and the racing of my heart.

The monster would keep me in the coop as punishment for not completing the chores and force me to watch their eyes shining at me. Then, staggering outside, bleating sheep would become zombies and turn to two legs for movement. Decaying animal corpses would become phantoms of the night. The blood would drip from other sacrifices in the killing shed, joining the puddle of congealed jelly under the drying and gutted fat lamb carcass. The dogs would hunt, digging up the buried offal, the kidney, the heart. Their jaws would be dripping and smeared. I would do anything to feel better, repetition, repetition, jobs and more jobs. I would hurt myself desperately vaulting fences, then stop and retrace as much as I could bear. The animals were out there somewhere. Some would want revenge for Dad killing their kind. I knew their eyes were following me and the hairs on the back of my neck would stand on end. I was terrified. I had seen helpless new-born lambs with their eyes pecked out by crows and blood leaking from their empty eye sockets, sometimes they were still alive. Perhaps I would be next, the son of the farmer taking the form of a ritualistic sacrifice. They were trailing me, each evening getting closer and increasing in number. I felt responsible for looking after the yard animals, if only the others would help. Didn't they understand how much needed doing? I was often not sure how I would eventually drag myself away, utter terror perhaps. I would be called into the house in time for grace before meals. My father would ask, "Paul, why are you late? You really are starting to frighten me."

The February sun was endless, soul destroying, impassive and merciless. It had no empathy. The lack of rain meant the sun's rays no longer brought pleasure, only hardship.

Tougher Love: Away 3 (March 1975)

Somehow, I settled myself into bed on my first night at the hospital, trapped in a room with three unknown faces. GP's merchandise may have helped. I didn't shower, no one cared. I was scared of showering and didn't wash for days. I remember I was next to Roy, the religious zealot. Bedtime was nine p.m. and he would pray loudly long after that. I prayed quietly to myself. GP had gone home. The night staff had moved in. I went to sleep thinking that I did not want to wake up.

I awoke the next day into my nightmare. I put my hands in front of my face and clicked my fingers as I had been taught to do, "One, two, three, wake up!" I said. I fully expected to be back in my own room, but I was still not in my own bed. I tried again, "One, two, three, wake up!" Where were my parents? Where was my family? Where was my home? No one was there to help me or talk to me, only strange people. Slowly, my country boy sense of the early morning kicked in. I pulled myself out of bed to dress in the clothes that Mum and Dad had left for me, black shorts, and a plain blue T-shirt. They had also bought me that beautiful new watch from a flash Perth jeweller. I felt proud putting it on. It was to become a symbol of identity.

I went downstairs to new people, new settings, new routines and a world of confusion. I was completely lost. Where should I go? What should I do? Walking a number of times through each doorway seemed the least of my problems. One younger patient asked me why I kept walking through doorways and what I was "in for." *Isn't it obvious?* I thought. I was Frankenstein's monster, the quintessential outsider. It made people not bother with me. They looked through and ignored me. GP was not in and everyone had their own concerns. There were no parents here, just strange adults, more concerned with the routine than the individual.

I was told I would not be going to school that day. I tried to get some breakfast and then I broke down, totally overwhelmed. I could not function. I could not do what I needed to. I had only one plan, to cry and yell until my parents came. Surely, they wouldn't leave me alone in this place. Somehow, I thought they would hear me. I wanted to be noticed and by God I would be. The more I was ignored, the more I howled. I sat on the steps shaking. Tears streamed down my face. "Mum, mum!" I cried. My mother was literally dead to me at that time. I became the little boy in the Nana Mouskouri song *Mamma,* facing the ultimate grief at a young age:

> And one little boy hears the doctor tell
> The others he thinks it's too late
> It's too late
> Mamma, he whispers quietly
> Mamma, you're looking old
> Mamma, why don't you answer me
> Mamma, your hands feel cold
> He rushes out into the chilly night
> He can't believe what he has been told

"Please, please, please!" I begged. "At least let me make a phone call." My throat became dry. I was dehydrated. I would ease off and then increase in volume again. They were long insistent cries. When I heard the noise, I told myself it was happening to someone else and then realised that it was coming from deep inside me. They were loud deep sobs of anguish. I wanted my family and begged for a phone call home. The students went off to school and for their part the morning shift ignored me.

I was not really concerned by the morning shift. We were trying to ignore each other, but as they went about their business, I did notice a surly male nurse called Cowan. He stood out as he did not seem to be very well received by the patients, and they exchanged poorly disguised ironic barbs. It was his arrogance, self-assured manner and condescending smile that seemed to set them off. His repartee with the boys seemed preoccupied with hardness and what it meant to be a man. He was overly intimate with the girls. If things got a little worse there would be "play" wrestling. I saw him that morning wrap his arms around a feisty Bruce, hurt him until he submitted, and then let him go with a vindictive laugh. He was strong and the patients were weak and in his arena. He was a younger nurse, although a little overweight, with a black moustache. The monster liked him. I felt it stir when he ambled passed with a pretentious swagger. They were allies, both searching for control and exploitation, the invitation, the crushing, and the final and complete destruction. He would give me furtive looks as he passed, shake his head, and finger his tie as if my wailing was a personal insult aimed at him alone. He also seemed particularly vindictive towards Rennie, calling him "Pretzel" and "Sissy" in his high-pitched nasal voice. There was some perception, suggested from the reaction of other staff that he had power. He was particularly clinical and dismissive of what he didn't like. I think he preferred quick outcomes. To him I was a box that had to be ticked. I made a mental note not to get in his sights as I wondered when GP would arrive.

During a break in my crying, as I sagged exhausted, with my head on my knees, one of the female nurses walked by. I would later learn that her name was Robinson and began to assume that the place was awash with them. She was older than Cowan. She was slim and had the nickname "Skinny Minnie." By contrast, there was a larger nurse who was also named Robinson, who was insultingly called "Fat Cat." Although this label was unflattering, it was a good way of differentiating between the two women as their natures seemed to complement their physiques. "Fat Cat" was relaxed and gregarious, to the point that she was very accepting of her nickname. "Skinny Minnie" was always fussing.

As my wailing continued, Cowan took offence. "That boy needs a lobotomy. He's playing Russian roulette."
"That's a little extreme, don't you think, Peter? He's just got here," Skinny Minnie chimed in.
"Well, he should be in the room at least."
"What do you think might be there for him? He's from the country for God's sake. Anyway, you can't do him without permission," she replied. I was shocked as they were right in front of me. Did they think I was some non-person, or a sheep?
Cowan continued, "Like they're going to know. At least we would have done something. He's so far gone now it's not funny. It's not like they're going to complain about it."
It occurred to me they were talking about my parents. "If not, he

can go to school. You're just going to put up with that crap, are you?"

Skinny Minnie gave him a penetrating look. "How can we send him to school like that? He'll go tomorrow anyway. You're not as important around here as you think you are, you know. Things can be changed with the stroke of a pen."

"Not by you," Cowan replied defiantly. "Let Peers give him some pills. He's good at that, even if he is a soft touch."

I don't recall much about the rest of the day other than wondering if I had entered an institution with the best practitioners, or ones using subtle sacrificial ritual. GP did not arrive until the afternoon when he once again began handing out medication at afternoon tea. I had not washed and barely eaten. Grimy tear tracks streaked my face and stained my clothes. I found the food strange and wondered, in any case, if I would keep it down. My throat felt red raw. This time I was medicated like the others. Cowan had a parting word as the shifts changed over. "Good luck with that one," he said, nodding towards me. "He was lucky he didn't go to the next step. I'll be watching."

GP looked at me and let out an exaggerated sigh. "I hear you've been a very naughty boy." I was confused by his tone. "Your merchandise will help, no need for anything else at this stage." He gave me some pills that I looked at suspiciously before swallowing.

Once again I begged to make a phone call and was finally allowed to. A sigh of relief and exhilaration went through my body. At last I could talk to my family, tell them things weren't working and to come and get me. I knew where the phone was. All my prayers would be answered. The pain of the day would be washed away. I knew the number as I often used the phone at home. I dialled with trembling fingers. I imagined it ringing in the hallway. To my horror, a foreign sounding accent answered my call. Who was this? I knew I had rung the correct number. I hung up in shock. I would later learn about the necessity of using an area code when ringing long distance. There was to be no phone call for me. I felt bamboozled and completely alone.

Dad: Home 4

It was the old axiom "Go west, young man!" that motivated Dad's family to leave their home in the beautiful South Australian hills surrounding Adelaide in 1955 and cross the Nullarbor Plain on unsealed roads. What's more, they did it in the family truck carrying all their belongings. Dad's father, Val, who bought and sold livestock, decided that there were more economic opportunities in the west and that the family of four sons, Vincent, the eldest, Eugene, John, Phillip, and daughter, Maureen, should all move. The purpose was to take advantage of the new opportunities in the west to increase their acreage. Dad's sister, Margaret, the firstborn, had died of pneumonia when she was thirteen.

Val's property had become too small to support the family and he persuaded his wife, Kathleen, a teacher at the small local primary school, to make the journey. Dad left his life of rabbiting, football, gymkhanas, shearing and general horseplay to make the trip. Uncle John, Dad's next younger brother, was lucky to be coming. As a youngster he had been playing "chicken" with Dad to see how many times he could cross the road before a car came. The pieces of him that were left over won the game and were rushed to hospital by Val and Kathleen. Dad told the story of how John was rushed to the hospital while being held in the arms of Kathleen in the back of the car while she implored her conservative husband to drive faster. At the hospital Val held his wife waiting for the news that they had lost another teenage child and sang to her:

> I'll take you home again, Kathleen
> Across the ocean wild and wide
> To where your heart has ever been
> Since you were first my bonnie bride.
> The roses all have left your cheek.
> I've watched them fade away and die
> Your voice is sad when e'er you speak
> And tears bedim your loving eyes.
> Oh! I will take you back, Kathleen
> To where your heart will feel no pain
> And when the fields are fresh and green
> I'll take you to your home again!

Miraculously John was sown back together and made a full recovery to chaperone one or two future Roses of Tralee. His claim to fame in later years was to become that he had rucked against AFL great Polly Farmer, and had his nose broken as Polly used his head as a stepladder for his knee.

Dad was very proud of and loved his life growing up in the Adelaide hills. I went back and visited the area once. Dad's friends would show me the rolling, lush hills that the Kain boys would walk over setting their rabbit traps. They told me there was not a lot of time for schoolwork as the family lived in a cramped shanty-style house and the early years were more about survival. I was also shown the unsealed roads the Kain boys would bounce over in their jalopies like kids on a trampoline. I viewed where they would ride their motor bikes and where they played rules football for the local teams. They learnt to be good horseman and participated in local gymkhanas. I even saw the famous drinking tree and heard the story of how Dad ended up escorting three charming young ladies to a community dance. Dad and his brothers were very proud of the night they changed all the signs around in their hometown. The police could never work out who was responsible. It was not all fun and games. He and at least one of his brothers became shearers and left to work on contract teams. In many ways the Kain boys were hard men.

On arrival in Western Australia the family kept driving until they found the rolling, arable fields of Narrogin to be to their liking for their future business. Dad and Uncle John went into partnership and purchased two adjacent farming properties on the outskirts of town. The early years were difficult in terms of meeting debt repayments, as to them it was a new kind of farming. Loans were difficult to get. They were rejected by most banks, but did business with an elderly central European lady, Mrs Starcevich, who had settled in town and owned property. In the end, they took out a loan with her instead of the banks. Dad told me the story of how at one point they were flat broke and could not meet the repayments on Uncle John's farm. They were forced to go to the old lady cap in hand to tell her she could not be paid until after the harvest. For them it was a humbling experience and a last resort. They had no legal recourse other than the goodwill of the lender. To their relief the terms were accepted. Dad and Uncle John always spoke fondly of the old migrant lady who had saved them from ruin and ending the farming empire before it had even begun.

Dad and Uncle John battled on to be respected as "true locals."

Mum termed them "Narroginites." They joined sporting clubs and became part of the social and agricultural scene. With their parents now living in the town they continued to practice their Catholic faith. They worked and played hard. In later years Dad and John became more settled and better farmers. They met good Catholic girls, married, had families, and continued in the farming business together.

On Friday nights after the family had been to the six o'clock mass Dad would stay in town to go to his drinking club. Mum would always be invited. "Why don't you bring the kids into the lounge and have a shandy?" She would mostly decline, and so the Friday night ritual would be in operation. It always struck me as somewhat ironic that you would take your family to mass as the caring father and then cross the street to overindulge in alcohol. Mum was always supportive of Dad having his "downtime" and didn't see it as hypocritical at all.

One night when I was about eight or nine, the whole family did go into the club and men would come and talk to Mum who looked radiantly beautiful. I approached Dad, some seven years older than Mum, shortish and bald, and asked, "How did you get to marry Mum?" I was suggesting he was punching above his weight. He looked at me with wide eyes as if he had been stung by a jellyfish.

"No worries, mate," he exclaimed in front of his fellow drinkers. Without missing a beat, he continued to help plan the farming arrangements on the town's boundaries.

Normally, several hours after being dropped at the club, Dad would phone to be picked up. Mum, my brothers, sister and I would pile into the car in our pyjamas for the fifteen minute drive into town. It seemed that we would wait for an eternity some nights. There wasn't much to do in the car. I knew why he was late and how it would be going. His mates would be playing games with him. "Just one more, Ewie," and Dad would stay. I was always mighty pleased to see him emerge through the large double doors of the club. Sometimes he would bring potato crisps as a "peace offering." On the way home he would lead us in a jovial saying of the rosary and comment to Mum, if she drove too slowly, that she should "try one of those other gears to see what it does."

Dad always loved sport as well as a beer. During our holidays down south, he took the family to the Packer cricket at Gloucester Park and as it was a hot day, imbibed freely. He then had to drive. Mum didn't like driving in the city. On the way home we called in to see Mum's parents near Fremantle, where Dad always looked to get on Grandpa's good side by sharing a long neck or two. Upon leaving, he was well and truly refreshed, perhaps too much as he proceeded to drive straight up the hill from Grandpa's flat, through a red light at the top and into oncoming traffic. In his defence, he was blinded by the setting sun, but he gave us all a hell of a fright. One minute I was examining my newly autographed cricket ball and the next I was torpedoed into the back of Mum's seat. Thankfully, we were all okay. Unfortunately, the damage to the car was significant and I remember the family walking reflectively back down the hill to our grandparents' place to spend the night. They must have got a bit of a surprise when we all landed, once again, on their doorstep.

It was a strange evening as there was only one spare room and we sunburnt children slept five across on the lounge room floor, having to put up with the comings and goings of the pet feline jumping nimbly between expensive looking ornaments on Grandma's shelf. I had just drifted off to sleep when I heard a loud bang, and the floor exploded with broken ceramics. I knew immediately that it was the cat. We had invaded his space and the inevitable had happened. I was about to turn on the light when I saw this large silhouette come hurrying in from the hallway. It was Dad. He was going to make amends and save us from what he thought was a low life city intruder. In the dim light I saw the silhouette pick up Simon's signed cricket bat and take a huge swing at where the sound had come from. There was another almighty crash and a shallow whimpered "mmeow." Dad had got the cat, and from the sound of it, a shelf lamp. The house lights came on. We looked at Dad and surveyed the destruction. There was the dazed and injured moggy, a broken ceramic with pieces on the floor, the shattered light and a bloodied stain on the sweet spot of the bat. He took it all in with a wry smile and commented, "Well, by God it was a beautiful cover drive."

Sputnik: Home 5

Dad and Uncle John had nicknames for everyone and everything. In fact, they created a separate language and identity list that could only be deciphered by someone with access to their secret code. The only problem was that to be in that group you needed to be given a moniker. For instance, Dad's farming neighbours knew about his names for them, so in turn he was christened "The Pope." The key to Dad's nicknames were that they were always ingenious and often contained a second level of meaning, which only the giver of the title was fully aware of and sometimes reflected apparently lesser-known personality traits or circumstances. He preferred references to public and historical figures and the military. It was like being inducted into a club when you were named and became part of the language. My nickname was "Corpy," or "The Little Corporal." I used to quite like it until I found out years later it had also been the nickname for Adolf Hitler. I questioned to myself if I had really been that regimented. He called Mum, "Bunny," which was a term of endearment and short for "Cream Bun." If he was worried about her putting on weight, he would call her "Buxom Bun." Jenny became known as "Pebbles" after *The Flintstones* character or "Jenny Wren." Simon was "Piemo," Grandpa was "The Boss," Nick was "Super Bingley" or "Super" and Uncle John named Danny "Wee Dapper Dan." They also had a code for animals. Sheep that were difficult or would not stay in their pen got it particularly hard. One of their favourites was "Madame Lafarge."

"Who was Madam Lafarge?" I curiously asked Dad one day. Unfortunately, he was in a fiery mood. His belt had snapped, and he was tying his pants with baling twine. He looked away in disgust, so Simon filled me in.

"She was a female character in the novel *A Tale of Two Cities* by Dickens. She used to sit and knit while she counted the heads of the nobleman that were guillotined during the French Revolution." *Okay, enough said on that one,* I thought. Badly behaved sheep could also be known as "Deer Foot the Shorn Ewe," which I think was a reference to American Indian culture and Dad's Hereford bull, Apex, even received a first name, "Haughty," after it won awards at The Royal Show. Unfortunately, the line between animals and people sometimes became blurred if you weren't careful.

Often the day would pass slowly on the farm. Dad and Uncle John went so far as to also give nicknames to things or events. Dad was a good bush mechanic, but he was sometimes too careful about making sure nuts didn't come off due to the personal and physical cost that might result in. Although a safe habit, it presented problems if you were trying to get the nut undone again, especially if you weren't Dad. Uncle John knew he had this bent and had his own classification for tight nuts that he passed on to his helpers. There was "tight," "very tight," "damn tight," and the most feared of all, "Ewie tight." More than once he and his boys were heard to complain in an exasperated fashion with barked knuckles and sweat dripping off their faces, "Yeah, that one's Ewie tight all right."

Of course, Dad got the blame for a lot of tight nuts that were not his fault, but Uncle John always rubbed it in by having a can of lubricant handy for show. In the end you had to be fully aware of the nicknames to communicate. If you walked into the morning tea conversation and heard that the Boss had gone home to see Bunny because he hurt his hand on the Ewie tight and Bingley was off chasing Madam La Farge, you might be more than a little confused.

The more unusual a nickname, the higher esteem you were held in. Farmhand and family friend, Rodney, must have been held in very high esteem indeed. He sometimes worked with Dad and Uncle John during the establishment of their business in the early 1960s, at about the same time as they got married and their wives started having children. Rodney had no strong family ties, so they were happy to "adopt" the younger man and give him a special place in their hearts. He was popular, tall, handsome and a good sort. He had earnt the handle "Sputnik," or "Sputty" for short. It was something us kids always wondered about when he came back to visit in the seventies, as he always looked fashionable and sophisticated. We knew Sputnik was the name of the first satellite put into space by the Russians in 1957, who in a surprise move, beat the Americans at their own game by initiating a first historical launch and starting a space race.

I also knew Dad was fascinated by the stars. When I was younger, I would often see him, on a clear night, walking out into the native Australian shrubs, beyond the shadows and the light that surrounded the house and looking skywards. One very still and moonlit night I braved the dark and skipped out. I was not fearful with my father beside me. There was not a breath of wind. I wondered if there was anything as fresh and clean as a dewy evening on a Great Southern sheep and wheat farm. I asked Dad what he was doing. "Just enjoying the beautiful clear air and stars. Right there, that's the Big Dipper," he would say with finality, and I would follow his finger into the blackness. "And that's the Southern Cross." This time, to my surprise, I could see the constellation he was pointing at. He would then ask me, "Can you see the archer?" I couldn't, and on this night, all I really wanted to know was the story of Sputnik, since Rodney had recently visited and Dad had used the name.

"And I suppose Sputnik is up there too somewhere, still orbiting around," I knew Dad would tell me the story. He loved stories.

"Ah yes, Sputnik, there's a story about that in regard to Rodney I can tell you." So I stood under the night sky, looking up at the heavens with my arm around my father in his golden brown dressing gown, while he told me the story of how Rodney Kent got the nickname of Sputnik.

In the early days of the farm we would have to work hard for a living. It was not always comfortable. We grew cereal crops, including oats. In fact, the farm still does. The thing with oats is that once dust is created it causes a rash and makes you itch like blazes. It's worse than a rash as it gets in your lungs, your hair, your eyes, cavities, and under your hat onto the scalp. It's abrasive and if you scratch it, you're gone, as the rash will spread. In those days, of course, there were no cabs on tractors; in fact, if you had an umbrella or an awning it was considered new age, so you were exposed to the sun and elements. You could not escape it in the truck, the bins or silos. Unfortunately, also due to the husky nature of the grain, it will only thresh in really hot conditions. The best you could do to combat it was to wear a sleeveless shirt and try to splash yourself down regularly. God help you if the day was windy. Of course, once you had harvested the oats the stubble would become sharp and cut your legs with tiny lacerations. You made every effort not to walk through it unless you really had to.

On this particular day I was up at the windmill next to the scrub trying to get some shade during our "smoko." It was always good to be near the water when you were harvesting oats. I had just given myself a big bath in the freezing brown water. It was so quiet after John had moved off with the tractor and harvester. The windmill was a Southern Cross. I looked up to see its great tin sails were rotating in what was quite a reasonable breeze. All I could hear was the pulling of the water as the mechanism was strained by the wind and reset, strain and stretch, strain and stretch. I was pleased that it was working well and filling the stock troughs nearby. The windmill was on top of the hill and looking down over a number of paddocks that were split by the creek in the gully. I could view the sheep trails running down to the troughs like patterns on a grid, always in unison.

John and I were operating the tractor pulled harvester. Rodney was collecting the grain in the old truck with a bin on the back. He didn't have a truck licence, so he could only drive on the farm. On the surface it seemed a better job, but the truck was stinking hot with the noon day sun beating down and like everything else, covered in itchy oats. It did have an air blower, but all it did on hot days was blow the oats dust around the cabin. Also, the oats had to be regularly shovelled in the truck's bin. This was the worst job of all, as you would be knee deep shovelling oats before taking it back to the silo to store. The only thing Rodney could do to cope was to have a smoke. It was not really the safest thing to be doing during the hot harvest days in the tinder dry paddocks.

I could see him slowly coming towards me in low gear, but at high revs, in the old International truck; it was about four tonne I suppose and difficult to drive with narrow gear gates at the best of times. He was smoking, as always, as he drove. Doubling the clutch was required, and with a load on there was a lot of stuttering and kangaroo-hopping as he tried to position the truck under the field bin auger. He already had half a load. I heard the gear box crack and shake as he dropped it back to first gear. He was a poor driver, but what happened next surpassed the mere lousy. Suddenly, I saw him grab frantically at his sleeveless shirt and accelerate straight past me. He looked like he had lost all control as he overshot the auger. His speed caused the bin to jump around as the tyres hit furrowed ground. To make matters worse, John was arriving back with the tractor and harvester ready to unload, working his jaw overtime as he always did when he was concentrating. Rodney was still in first gear, but heading out into the stubble with half a truckload of grain and the engine screaming. In panic, I jumped up and took off after him into it. I could feel it grazing my legs as I ran, but this was an emergency. As I got closer, I could hear his alarmed cries. Something was definitely amiss. Meanwhile, John had done a U-turn in the tractor and was bouncing after us as well. Thankfully, the old International wasn't going too quickly. When I got level with him and looked in the window, I saw a strange sight. Rodney was on fire. I saw smoke under his shirt and perhaps a flame or two. He had forgotten all about steering and had both hands off the wheel. His foot was jammed on the accelerator in what must have been a reflex action. "The brake, Rodney!" I stammered; I had run nearly to the point of exhaustion. "Pull the handbrake!" He took his foot off the accelerator at this point, and I could see the quick movement of his arms. I noticed he was gyrating and trying to take his shirt off. I jumped up on the running board, reached in and pulled the handbrake. The truck stalled and came to a stop in a cloud of dust from the ploughed land and the oats from the bin. He still seemed to be in a great deal of pain.

"My smoke..." he gasped as he jumped out of the truck. "It's burning me." While literally ripping off his shirt he skedaddled for the dam at a quick pace, leaving me to scratch my head and not just because of the oats. I looked inside the cabin and could smell burning. My suspicions were confirmed when I picked up the smouldering fabric. It turned out that his burning cigarette butt had fallen down the front of his open shirt. It combined with the itch and rash from the oats dust to cause extreme pain and panic. I looked over at John, who was doubled over laughing. Once the shock had worn off and I realised there had been no real damage done, I joined in with him. In fact, we laughed until we cried. It had been a boring, hot day and we enjoyed the humour and relief.

"Well, Rodney really went into orbit that time," John said at last wiping back a tear.

"Yep, just like Sputnik," I added. The name was to stick to Rodney like glue. He had performed his rite of passage. We walked back to the dam and John patted Rodney, who was now sitting soaking on the dam bank. He seemed okay, apart from a few superficial marks.

"You all right, Sputnik?" John asked. "By the way that's your new nickname. I reckon you've earned one."

"I don't suppose you two old buggers are going to give a young coot any sympathy?" he stammered.

"Not likely," I responded. "You are now Sputty, otherwise known as the man who goes into orbit." From that day on it was my job to always remind him about the dangers of smoking on the job.

Dad had been so entertaining with the telling of his story I had forgotten that we were outside in the dark. "I think you were hard on Sputnik. Are you certain you're not pulling my leg?" I asked, suppressing a quiet annoyance.

"No way, Corpy," he responded as we went back to the house. "That story is ridgy didge as witnessed by significant persons."

Years later Sputnik was to be a pallbearer at Dad's funeral. I was next to him as we put his coffin in the grave. I swear I could hear him calling out to Rodney: "How's the oats harvesting going, Sputnik? Don't smoke in the itchy oats, will you, son."

School: Away 4 (March 1975)

I didn't sleep well that night knowing I would be starting at a new school the next day. I wasn't aware at the time, but I was not to miss any days of school at Graylands Primary, partly because I wanted to prove that the accusations that I was a school avoider were not true. It was true that I was not happy at school, but I believed the box that said I was a school avoider should not have been ticked. As an adult I would discover that school abstaining was always a critical legal factor in child guardianship and monitoring. I felt with me it was manipulated to achieve an end.

I awoke that morning to the sound of Roy going through his copious prayer ritual and being shouted down by the others in the dorm. *This guy is even worse than me*, I thought. I noted what would happen if I lay on my bed praying Hail Marys. I had not yet found what I perceived as the courage to pray aloud, and in fact, never would. This was, in actuality, probably good. I would feel aggrieved that Roy would leave the hospital much earlier than me even though I didn't succumb to my public prayer compulsions. In fact, all the patients in the hospital would leave before me. Did this mean that I was the craziest or just the most forgotten? Was I to be held up as an example of what would happen if you didn't toe the line?

My parents had not yet returned with my school clothes, so I was to front up in my black shorts, pulled high, and my plain blue T-shirt. I managed to avoid Rennie as he literally flew down the corridor shouting, "We're all on a plane to Poofter's Paradise." I suppose by that he meant the bus to school. Suddenly, there was an ominous thud from one of the single rooms and a wail that I thought could only be that of a tortured soul.

"I told you, I'm not going." I popped my head into one of the single rooms and saw a very strange sight. One of the biggest boys in the hospital was lying on the bed, gripping it fiercely, while being dressed for school by three male nurses.

"Fucking get off. I hate school."

"Don't make us carry the bed downstairs," one of the nurses was saying. "Because we will."

"And all the way to the school bus, if necessary," another chimed in.

"You're fucking killing me," he screamed. "I'll just run away."

Upon reflection I can see why I didn't miss any days at school while I was at hospital. At the time I wondered if this was a daily occurrence. The screaming continued. It was an intense struggle, but eventually the nurses won the "Battle of the Bedroom" due to weight of numbers, but lost the war as I hardly saw this fellow again. *Now that*, I thought to myself, *is a school refuser.*

Somehow the staff got us fed and I had a little breakfast. Then it was time for final organisation and down to the bus. It seemed to be an ordeal even to get to school and very different to what I was used to. The family school routine at home was much more orderly. Catching the big green MTT bus for the short ride was a new adventure. I had never caught public transport before. It would run past the enormous Karrakatta cemetery that gave the impression of taking up a whole suburb. To this day, I still love the experience of being driven and find the big green buses soothing, especially the older style ones that are now so rare. Emotionally, a green bus for me was like the lights of a nearby ship as you bobbed lost in the ocean. I also liked them because I always felt that travelling was achieving something. You begged them not to pass, but they always did and left you only with the memory and the feeling.

So began my first day, when once again I found myself in the office of somebody important; this time it was the principal, tall and unsmiling in his brown suit. I was introduced and chatted to briefly before being led to my Year 5 class. I did not think things could get any worse, but I was wrong.

Mum: Home 5

When I was about thirteen, Mum took her five children to the visiting circus in Narrogin. It was the first time we had been to a circus and came about because we got free tickets. We were sitting near the front. It was a good performance. We were having a great night. It got even more interesting when the clowns came on. In this act they were looking for a volunteer from the audience, "a pretty lady," in fact. We knew we were safe because Mum would sooner crawl through a pig sty than volunteer at a circus. Unfortunately, she had not anticipated the tenacity of this particular clown. He walked around and around the big top looking for a volunteer until he stopped in front of Mum and stared awe struck. "OOOH, pretty lady," he announced to the audience after a long silence. He had found what he had been looking for. It sent the crowd, and in particular, my siblings and I, into hysterics. The "pretty lady" then became a centrepiece of his performance. He would go into his routine, have the audience in the palm of his hand and suddenly stop, turn in our direction, and call out to Mum, "Hey, pretty lady."

Simon leaned across and whispered in Mum's ear, "Mum, can you stop being so beautiful, you're distracting the clown." That's the way it was with Mum's children. We thought she was beautiful because she was our mother, not just because the clown said so. It was no surprise to us at all that she was picked out.

Josephine O'Connell was the second eldest of thirteen children.

I grew up with a lot more aunts and uncles than most kids. Her father, Brian, was a high-ranking government civil engineer whose family had connections with C.Y. O'Connor, who was responsible for the Goldfield's water pipeline. He was eight years older than my grandmother. He married and had Nellie Hair in child when she was only seventeen, thus causing some unrest with both connections. He came from a deeply religious Catholic family with several vocations to the sisterhood. Some of Mum's siblings were highly successful in the professional world, with roles including the Chief Engineer of the iconic new parliament house, and Chief Executive Officer of the CAA. Grandpa did not place a lot of academic pressure on his daughters. He believed it was a patriarchal world. This attitude reached a head as he began to have children in a desperate effort to have sons to carry on the family name. His first four offspring were all females, and he would comment to anyone who asked after the birth of his fourth consecutive daughter about the gender of the child, that it was "another bloody girl." Thankfully, after that he became the proud father of a spate of boys.

Mum and her family grew up in Waroona on the southwest highway between Perth and Bunbury, and then Albany. She had a charm that made her stand out. She was a good school student. Tall and athletic, she was a notable tennis and netball player. Her mother, Nellie, raised her as a lady and she became proficient in the violin. She would sometimes play serenades by Brahms in performance, with her alluring pale white complexion and fashionable fifties hair style stealing the show. After leaving school, she began work in bookkeeping, something that was to hold her in good stead for running the farm finances after marrying Dad. She was also active in the community. Her beautiful smile and glamorous good looks helped her win beauty contests in Albany. It was about then that she met handsome Eugene Kain who used to visit Albany to represent Narrogin, some six hours away, at Great Southern football carnivals. It was the beginning of a long-distance courtship. Dad, some seven years Mum's senior, would take time off from working on the farm to make the trip to Albany, where he would beg Mum to give him a "peaches and cream" smile. They were married in Albany in March 1962 and Josephine, or Jo, moved to be with her new husband on the farm named "Cooramining," about fifteen minutes out of Narrogin in Western Australia's wheatbelt.

Mum was not happy in her new home at first, saying she didn't fit in with her "Narroginite" husband and his social set. She once again had inherited a man's world. Eugene would often go off to parties some miles away and leave her at the farmhouse by herself. She was lonely at night when he was away and sometimes frightened. There were problems with black and brown snakes, spiders, an outside laundry and toilet, no scheme water and electricity supplied by a generator. The outside laundry was a favourite haunt for snakes. They would also slither across the grass at the front of the house. Dad would shoot them with the shotgun when they were found and hang them on the water storage tank next to the laundry. It was a long way from the glamorous accolades of being a beauty queen and the aesthetic comforts of Albany. Thankfully, it was not long before children came along, starting with Simon, myself, eighteen months later, and then my only sister, Jennifer. It was about this time that Mum miscarried.

Simon was four, and I suppose, starting to follow Dad around on his daily farm chores. Mum had her hands full with me, aged two, and Jenny, ten months. She was without support from her family and assistance from the town was minimal. It could not have been easy raising three young children at an isolated farmhouse. She later realised she was probably suffering from postnatal depression, rarely diagnosed as it was in the sixties. She was pregnant with a fourth child when it all became too much. Dad was often supportive and helpful with the children, but he was busy completing the spring work tasks and must have simply told her to "pull yourself together." It was a beautiful brisk morning. The breeze blew and there was a light frost on the spring shoots and tall green grass. The refreshing morning hid the torrent of sadness and the valley of tears that were building up inside Mum.

Physically and emotionally, things were not quite right. In desperation she cranked up the old wooden blower and got connected to Uncle John's wife, Diane. She was busy with her own young children, but would make the ten minute trip a little later in the day. After hanging up, she rang her local GP, Dr Zilko. He recognised her distress and booked her in immediately. She dressed for town. There was not much the doctor could do. His only comfort was to say that it might be "for the best." She walked out of the surgery and for some reason thought she could hear a dog barking some distance away. Her world stood still. She did not see the townsfolk or notice the cars on the road, but drove very slowly to the Catholic church and uttered a silent prayer for her unborn child, my sibling, the empty bed between Jennifer and Nicholas. She arrived home to find Jenny in her little frock trying to stand for the first time in her playpen. Not bearing to have to sit down and think, she went outside, and walked, quietly sobbing, around the house.

Her thoughts wandered to her time as a waitress in the eastern states. She remembered the hustle and bustle of swanky downtown Melbourne in her early twenties and how much she enjoyed working at the plush Windsor Hotel, where the cream of Australian society frequented. The ladies stepped out in their best fashions and clients tipped well and were most always appreciative. She became known for her grace and beauty as she danced between guests like a butterfly. She was asked for and in demand. She enjoyed her work and was valued. She thought of a polite and charming older couple. Well spoken, they would ask for Mum every Saturday night for three months or so. She would serve them their evening meal. They tolerated being upset by a surly gentleman who dined across the room and often leered at them, maintaining their dignity at all times. She remembers they were sad to see her go and left a large tip for what she had done and for making their weekend evenings so pleasant. A polite hug and a kind word were exchanged as they departed. The man spoke, "Thanks so much for your service, Josephine, and I don't know how you put up with that horrible Mr Evatt who was always glaring at us."

"Thank you, Sir Robert and Dame Pattie." Josephine said goodbye to Australia's longest serving Prime Minister and his wife and was left to look after the future President of the UN General Assembly without their intestinal support.

Homework: Away 4 (March 1975)

I arrived home from school exhausted and with a much fuller bag than when I set out that morning. I slumped through the barrier door with the other patients and into my developing nightmare. GP was there to greet us with pills and afternoon tea. "You look like you've had a hard day, Boss. Take some of these and you'll feel better." I took the medication he handed me. "Grab a biscuit and something to drink and come with me." I followed him into one of the small rooms at the back of the living area and sat down. "How did school go?" he asked. I burst into tears. He gave my back a little rub.

"I've got so much homework," I said and took out my new maths book to show him. "Miss Noske gave me twenty pages of fractions to catch up on in one night." I went through the pages she had marked. GP looked like he had been given an electric shock. I was embarrassed that the pages stunk of biro ink. "I can't do twenty pages," I said and put my head in my hands. "And it's maths. School is awful. It's full of poms from the hostel."

"Surely that's not a big deal," GP offered.

"There's just so many of them. All they talk about is soccer and the girls keep calling ants "unts."" GP had a laugh at that.

"You must have met someone you liked."

"Well, Rex showed me around the school, he's Aboriginal. He told me he survived Cyclone Tracey." Cyclone Tracey had devastated Darwin the previous Christmas. In actual fact, Rex had only stood on the grass quadrangle in the middle of the school and answered my requests as to where the facilities were with a nod of his head, in what could have been any direction, and the briefest of replies, "Ober der," or "Up der," and if I was lucky, actually pointed something out. It was as if the locations were so plainly obvious no more guidance was required.

"I met Mr Viska who's been everywhere and Mr R who hands out spelling lists if you talk. I was caught talking, but he let me off with a warning. There was a strange health teacher who seemed fascinated about what I wrote about cleaning my teeth and I had to read it to the class."

"What did you do at breaks?" GP asked. I looked up forlornly and shrugged.

"Not much," I replied.

"You need to tell me, Paul. I can't help if I don't know what's going on."

"I… I went and hid in the toilets," I reluctantly stammered. I felt myself reddening. Gordon was my only friend. I didn't want him to know I was a loser. "What do you expect? You know I don't have any friends at that school."

"Well, you should make friends. I suppose it's only your first day. Did you stay there the whole time?"

"I found a quiet spot outside the Year 7 classroom and sat on the walkway and cried."

"That's not very good, is it?"

"A few students asked me why I was crying and if I wanted to play. Which was nice, I suppose."

"I'm sure you can do better than that. Tomorrow is another day."

"That's what I'm worried about." I don't think that's what GP wanted to hear. "Everybody will still be there I suppose," and I added as an afterthought, "if they haven't committed suicide."

GP looked shocked. "I don't think you should mention suicide around this place. There are folks that are suicidal. We give them pills for it. I don't think you really know what you're talking about and it's a subject that shouldn't be taken lightly. People need to know that once they make that decision it's over for them. There's no coming back and it's family and friends that are left to carry the burden."

"Is that why some parents are always here giving gifts? Are they trying to buy off their kids and stop them running away?"

"And don't even think about running away." GP was quite firm. "It will just add time to your sentence." He had realised that I saw my time in hospital as being like jail.

"Everybody else does," I replied. I got a look that killed and changed my tack "Where would I run to? I don't know anyone in the city. I don't know how to get home."

"That's good then. As long as we understand each other." I realised later that they probably couldn't have done much if I had run away, as patients tended to leave after the event. It was true though that as a ten-year-old from the country I didn't really have the resources or know how to return from the city. GP led me back out and I followed like one of Dad's sheep.

I opened my school bag and got out my maths homework. The first page took me about fifteen minutes. I thought of the other nineteen pages and burst into tears. "I won't do this," I wailed. "It's not fair. Nobody else has to do this. It's not fair," I put my head in my hands. Cowan had just arrived for the shift changeover. He did not miss the opportunity. His nostrils flared and he addressed GP.

"Will you shut him up, Peers? He's upsetting everybody again. You know what should be done. You know where he should be going."

"You know you can't do that, Mr Cowan," GP replied with uncertainty in his voice. He then spoke directly to me. "It's okay, Paul. It doesn't matter if it's not done. We'll work something out." I couldn't cope and continued to whimper loudly. Cowan was clearly agitated and had a bee in his bonnet. He came and stood over me. He was close enough that I could smell his tobacco breath. I felt intimidated. I definitely could not work now.

"Actually, I'll see if I can give him a hand," he said with a barely disguisable leer. "You go, Peers. It's time for your changeover."

"I suppose it is," GP replied. "Don't do anything stupid will you?" With that he made for the barrier door, and I presumed, checked out. I was alone with Cowan. His manner changed to a more aggressive one as he spoke to me.

"Okay, Pretzel, I think I've got something that will help with that homework. Follow me."

I felt uneasy, but picked up my maths book and followed. I wasn't sure at first where we were going, but it soon became clear it wasn't to a better situation. We stepped through the main corridor and into the side hall that I had asked questions about when I first arrived. Cowan took out an unfamiliar, but clearly marked key. It was larger than the others. "How is this helping with my maths homework, Mr Cowan?" I asked tentatively.

"I don't know about helping you, but it's certainly going to help everyone else, me included." I was about to reply when I saw the door he was unlocking. It was not the door marked "No Admittance," but the one next to it that I hadn't ever seen inside. The hairs on the back of my neck stood up and I froze like an icicle. A red haze of stress filled my brain and moved down to my shoulders. It was as if a torment I once had was coming back to haunt me. The room that he had opened was small and completely stark, with what appeared to be white cushioning on all walls. It stunk of antiseptic. "In you go, buddy," Cowan sneered. He gave me a good shove in the back.

Jenny: Home 6

On the day I interviewed Jenny at her house in coastal Bunbury, she was dressed casually. She was looking very thin, as always, in a loose, cotton checked green shirt and she wore no shoes. She was an enthusiastic participant in the interview and was smiling, although I knew she would become emotional later on. She had the female Kain clan handsomeness, fully flushed cheeks and had inherited some of her mother's good looks. Like her she was quite tall, although lacking in her elegance. Her looks were on myself and Danny's side of the family. Her second name of "Mary," in the traditions of good Catholicism, was a reference to the Virgin Mary, and as the only daughter, a no-brainer. Mum had brought her up to be a lady and Jenny had in later times became her confidant and proxy carer as she aged. I reminded her of the family anecdote where she had had a vivid dream as a twelve-year-old and called out in her sleep, "Oh it's a wedding." Dad had heard her and often reminded her of the story. Perhaps Jenny had sought to never fall into the "wedding trap" as a result. She was the apple of her father's eye and loved him too, but may have harboured some resentment about his intimidation of male suitors, indicated by once giving him an "American Gothic" birthday card and explaining bluntly why. Her brothers were also overprotective as they did not want to lose their only sister to a male "predator." In any case, Jenny loved weddings. She had attended many and often participated in them with her lovely singing or reading.

Dad loved, but was overly protective of his daughter. The event of the Year 12 ball after party at the farm shearing shed highlighted this. He was worried about his daughter and wanted to keep an eye on her, enough to take responsibility for hordes of excited teens to descend on his property at night. There was to be no "funny business." In fact, after the party started, he put a lock on the gate and would not let anyone leave until they convinced him they had not been drinking. In some cases, his puritanical whim could only be satisfied by having the driver breath on him. He raised even more eyebrows in the early hours of the morning with the arrival of the farm truck, fully equipped, harbouring the cattle cage on the back. Those sitting on the shed veranda at four a.m. in the morning must have checked what was in their drink as they saw the silhouette of the monolith coming at them through the darkness of the farm slopes with the headlights blazing. Dad then herded all the "heifers," including his daughter, into the truck and whisked them away to the farmhouse for the rest of the night, thus confining the disappointed males to celibacy.

My chat with Jenny was important as she was the only female child. She was also a close sibling and had taught at some of the same schools I had. I talked with her about her recent fiftieth birthday and who had attended. "Simon didn't come, of course. I see him so rarely these days." Her dislike of her older brother was well known in the family. We moved the conversation on to other matters. "You know, I'm thinking about writing my own blog," she commented brightly. "I don't think anyone will read it, but I would just like to do it for the experience." I asked her what the recollections of the time just before I went away to hospital were.

"Leading up to the hospitalisation, you were behaving very strangely. I noticed you walking steps backwards and forwards, doing things like turning light switches on and off and having to walk in circles. It was obviously... well nothing was obvious to me at that time because I was just a child... I have trouble remembering things from my childhood, but I remember Mum and Dad took you to Perth and we (the children) went to Aunty Diane's. We knew you weren't doing that well you know... we sort of hoped that it would be fixed. Sometimes, Mum offered, or you got her, to complete rituals for you and this tired her out." Jenny was close to Mum and recognised her pain.

"I could tell that she just wasn't coping and also needed help and support. She blamed herself and took pills for anxiety. You know, in hindsight, it would have been better if you had stayed with the family, but there was a lack of resources. When you went away to hospital I was scared and I'm sure my other brothers had a secret fear that they would be taken away. We all missed you after you left and were shocked when we woke up one morning and found you weren't there. Mum had actually cooked you breakfast. She broke down and cried. It was the only time I ever saw her breakdown. She was devastated and we were devastated because we didn't know what the outcome was going to be."

Jenny then turned to her recollection of my actual time at the hospital from her point of view: "Dad was, of course, stoic. He tried to support Mum as much as he could, but he fell back on his religion... it had to do with the way the family was brought up with isolation and socialisation issues involved with being on the farm." Jenny had memories of the family's regular trips to Perth to see me: "I think if it wasn't every weekend, it was every second weekend. You would know better than us. We shut things out too. I do remember being really glad to see you… but I do have a really horrific memory of one particular time we visited you. We had been playing out the back and on this particular time when the family went to leave, you kicked out and you were stretched against the window, and you wouldn't let us leave and it was very traumatic for everybody. I do remember that very clearly… I don't think children should be taken away from their families. It can be very hard to deal with for the kids… kids are victims of their emotions and sometimes their actions are just a cry for help."

The Padded Cell: Away 6 (March 1975)

I went sprawling against the soft cushioned walls. I could not keep my balance and landed face first. Once again, I asked myself if this was really happening. It was a padded cell. It was freezing and I tasted bile in my mouth. I felt nauseous and broke out in a cold sweat despite the cold. I was having a panic attack. There were fingernail marks gouged in the walls and tufts of material hung out here and there. What did Cowan think I was going to do to myself for heaven's sake? I know I was upset, but this was completely over the top. Instead of Cowan, I saw the monster, its fangs glistening with saliva, drips forming a puddle at its feet. I could smell the stench of its breath as its tiny spider minions fled the room, as if not being able to face what happens next. I waited for the door to close with a crash and the heavy bolt lock to be put in place. Suddenly, in the doorway I saw GP. He had the light behind him. He reminded me of a guardian angel. I suppose in this case he was. "Get out, Paul," he said curtly. "You don't need to be in there." I came out on GP's request. He was looking darkly at Cowan and there was clearly a standoff between the two.

"I thought you'd left for the day, Peers," Cowan said with a vicious sneer.

"Well, it's just as well I hadn't, isn't it? I thought I would perhaps stay a while to keep an eye on things. What do you think you're playing at, Cowan? This is not in his treatment. He's my patient."

"You know how Dr Robinson feels about the sort of behaviour he was showing. I was using my initiative."

"I know all about your use of initiative and the skulls on the wall that result, sooner if not later. I'm sure Williams would be interested in your actions."

"Williams!" he laughed. "Knock yourself out. You know I just need to make a phone call to put things right." He paused. "It looks like I'll have to wait until you're gone then."

GP raised his voice and fixed a glare at Cowan. "Don't ever take him near that room again." Then he spoke to me. "Let me know, Paul, if Mr Cowan ever tries to repeat this episode. He doesn't have the authority."

Cowan was smirking. "Well, spin the revolver and take your chances, Peers. You have to go home sometime and when you come back he might not quite be the person, if you could call it him that, that he is now. There's a lot more things we can do around here you know instead of just filling folks full of pills. I'm more of a doer myself. There's next door for instance."

GP put his collar up and gave him a long cool stare. He had his motorcycle jacket on ready to go home and could look tough when he wanted to. "Well, pity next door if I have to put you in there." Cowan coughed and slunk away like a snake. When it came down to it, he was a coward, and I guess needed bullying to be put in his place. I envisioned him as a marionette, helpless on a stage with Dr Robinson pulling his strings. "You okay?" GP asked me. "I can give you something if you like."

I had started off with a homework problem and now I had been assaulted, but I knew it could be much worse. "Thanks, but I'm okay," I offered at last. I wished GP could do more to reinstate my confidence in the adult world.

"Maybe take a break from your homework. I'll talk to your

teacher." I felt as if a great weight had been lifted from my shoulders. "Let me know too if you're not sleeping. I can give you something for that. Miss Raatz is taking a group to the movies on Saturday to see *Young Frankenstein* in the city and I want you to be able to go."

"Who's Miss Raatz?" I asked.

"You'll find out soon enough, Boss," he said. The conversation ended abruptly.

Simon: Home 7

Again, and again and again and again,
Why don't you do it, why don't you do it again?

And so, the lyrics of the well-known and catchy *Status Quo* song vibrated at high decibels throughout the Kain boys' den, otherwise known as "the bunkhouse." It was christened the bunkhouse by four billets who stayed over from an underage Queensland cricket team that visited our town. It was a very comfortable arrangement for boys. It had been built several years after my return from Stubbs Terrace to house myself and my three brothers and give Jennifer privacy and space in our old bedroom. It was a non-architecturally designed double brick square room built on a raised slab connected to the house by a concrete walkway that smelt of mouldy boots, most of which congregated in the new shower recess that seemed like a great idea at the time, but for obvious reasons of privacy, was seldom used. It became a room dominated by a table tennis table and then a pot-belly stove and strewn with essential equipment of tween boys growing up on a farm: one or two desks, bookshelves, a dartboard, air rifles, footballs, posters of idols, a record player, cricket bats and equipment, motorcycle helmets, in fact, anything that made boy life more palatable. The windows looked out onto the back lawn, or as we liked to call it, our house cricket pitch. It was actually more our show ground, like the SCG 2, as we had concrete nets for more formal battles. The room had cheap durable carpet and cheaper beds, up to eight of them, with room for a number more, but to us it had heaps of style.

This style was mainly older brother Simon's, as evidenced by the loud exposure to his favourite music. He had discovered *Status Quo* when asked to complete an assignment on a rock band at school. This led to an obsession that saw him acquire every album the group ever produced. If we went shopping and found a new music store, Simon would always ask for a *Status Quo* album he didn't have. I would pray that they would have it so his obsession would be sated. Mum called the group *Quo Vadis*, a reference to a famous biblical movie that hinted at where she would rather have his interest. My brothers and I were raised on *Status Quo* and knew the title of every album and the lyrics of every song. We only had a seventies record player, but we rigged up some speakers and got some decent sound happening. It was his way of letting those in the den offer homage. Simon introduced me not to the latest fashions, but to personal style. It had not always been this way. King Simon had not always been this way.

Very few people at first meeting picked Simon and I for brothers. We did not look alike. We were about the same height, but we had different noses and complexions. I had inherited the O'Connell nose and his was Roman. His features were flat, and he was big framed with freckles. I was blonde in appearance and skin tone with a lighter frame. Simon had a similarity in looks to Nick, while Jennifer, Daniel and I were out of the same pod. Nick and Simon also had different personalities. They were more down to earth. In regard to the looks and behaviours of us siblings, there appeared to be two sides to the family.

He was in Grade 7 during my suffering in 1975. When I returned, he had morphed into a leader and a personality. He had become

"Slimy Man" or "The Torpedo," a reference to his aggressive fast bowling in cricket. I knew all about it as I had been facing it in our backyard for years and was probably why I was never intimidated by fast bowlers. He played up to expectations. Very muscular for his age and good at sport, he had the skills and values that primary school aged children were looking to emulate in a country town and to feel good about. Girls experiencing the early pangs of teenage hormones would signal him out as "the one" and giggle when he walked past. At school in the years leading up to 1975, I often used to sit in my favourite spot and watch him, and as it appeared to me, the other heroes of Grade 6 and 7. Simon was not academic, but loved to read westerns and occasional classics. One of these was Alexandre Dumas' *The Man in the Iron Mask*. I noticed his interest in the book and asked him about the meaning of the title when he was reading it, being of a younger age I didn't fully comprehend it. He replied that one day I would understand it. Of course, it was the infamous story of the French king who kept his brother locked up and unrecognisable so he could not contend as the heir to the throne. I would later ask myself the question: Was I like the man in the iron mask?

My favourite spot was behind the toilet block in the area that caught the morning sun, where the Grade 1 to 4 students could play. Sometimes I would play in the designated junior playground, but I gave it a break after Eddie O'Reilly offered to put a drill bit into the penis of all the males in junior school who frequented it. Narrogin was far inland and in a valley. The mornings were brisk and fresh in late autumn and winter, and that was before the freezing breeze blew. Long school shorts were compulsory, and our jumpers were thin. It was cold enough inside the classroom if you were at the wrong end for the heater, but life outside the classroom was sometimes not a normal cold. Our teeth chattered and our skin goose pimpled as if it was rubbed with ice to become pink and raw. It was a constant search for warmth. It didn't occur to me that I might get warmer more quickly if I was moving around.

The action took place in "The Big Boys' Playground" or gravel pit. Even its name, promoting "big boys," established an expectation. It was about fifty metres long and thirty metres across and surrounded on two sides by a waist high ring lock and wood fence that could be easily jumped over to retrieve lost balls or hide a late entrance to school. At playtime it normally housed about forty boys. It was also a thoroughfare into the massive convent, a once busy iconic monolith that now only housed a quarter of the nuns it was intended for, and the special school. The playground slanted down the hill with a hint of bitumen at the top by the goal-sized entrance where vehicles accessed. The slant was an obvious advantage for any team kicking down the incline. The bottom fence line ran parallel with the main road into town. You could see the playground of the government primary two hundred yards in the distance. Quarry like in colour, it contained not a blade of grass during summer and had a clay base, hardened by many years of hot summer sun. Anything resembling onion weed was trampled after the first session of the term. It was not a place where boys chatted, ate amiably under trees or sat on benches talking of secret societies. That might come later after you had proven your manhood. It was a world where "doers" were king. Instead, the trees and benches were part of "the stadium," and there was a technique involved in working around them.

In the mid-seventies, the school was struggling financially and for numbers. It was a difficult environment and school attitudes, despite the connection to Catholicism, followed the rule of "survival of the fittest." Simon prospered in the pecking order. I wished I was like him. Indeed, I received accolades for just being his brother. The truck width gateway and large cylindrical metal posts at the entrance to The Big Boys' Playground reminded me of the entrance to Hades, the Greek underworld. The three-headed guard dog, Cerebus, was personified by a number of prowling senior school students who would give short shrift to any juniors who wanted to come down before their time in an attempt to enhance their manhood. You hoped you would walk back through the gates after the sound of the bell, having proven your heroism once again. I imagined the sign on the gates: "Abandon all hope ye who enter." Once you had passed through those gates you crossed the white line, and anything went. There was British Bulldog, Red Rover All Over and Aussie rules football matches, where the only way to get a free kick was by mutual agreement of both sides, if you were still fit enough to take it. The dog-eat-dog culture was powerful and exacerbated at the time by students that were state athletes, and one that would represent Western Australia in AFL. Like Simon, to me and others, these boys were heroes to be looked up to. It was important you prove your worth to them. In short, it made cage fighting look like *Andy Pandy*. I think the nuns were always thankful that the do gooders and debaters didn't often take an interest in the boys' yard. If they did, they would have the line quoted to them, "that boys will be boys." Well, they certainly were in The Big Boys' Playground.

The attitude of the teachers to The Big Boys' Playground reminded me of the supervision requirements of the prisoner's recreation yard I came across when I visited Fremantle Prison after it closed. I could relate to its status as a prison of punishment. In the recreation yard the prisoners split into a number of cliques, for instance, the bikies or indigenous, and would huddle for protection. The warders would view the events from behind a small wire enclosure at one end of the yard, and due to their intensity, change over every thirty minutes. If someone was being killed or seriously assaulted, an alarm would be rung. At The Big Boys' Playground, they would probably forget the alarm and just wait for the students to return to class. There were no male teachers in the school. Woe betide any petite female who tried to do something other than observe from outside the fence.

On the day of the vicious stone fight, when the boys spent thirty minutes throwing pieces of gravel at each other and two students received serious eye injuries, not a teacher entered the scene. The only way to survive was to get someone before they got you. Family members and clans formed small groups with their backs to the fence all over the playground. It was utterly terrifying. I saw a student go down, clutching his precious eye, as the battle went on in all corners. The stone had been thrown from my clan, someone only yards away.

Afterwards, all the students were assembled and any boy who had held a stone was lined up and caned in front of the cohort. The rest of the students watched with bated breath as the heroes were punished. The truth was that they probably needed to be every day. It was a hard way to learn that my brother was not a god.

Young Frankenstein: Away 7 (March 1975)

"My oath I would!" I replied when Miss Raatz asked a group of patients if they wanted to go to the movies. I wondered if this was to be my first date with a city girl. I did not really believe in puppy love, so I didn't think I was in love with Miss Raatz. I resolved that I would go as long as I wouldn't think much about her after I left hospital and never really wonder what became of her. In fact, it was my first touch of city emotion, or at least the fascination of attraction for the opposite gender. If I was not in love with her, I decided, I was not in love with anybody else. She was like an exotic flower that I planted that I mistakenly thought I could grow and would soon wither and die due to my poor treatment of it. Afterwards, I would feel empty and angry at my unbridled extravagance and wonder what I had been thinking.

I could not blame myself too much. She was difficult to resist. She was one of the youngest nurses and beautiful. I was fascinated by the juicy details she would "leak" about her personal life. I knew she lived with two men. To my ten-year-old mind that was totally appropriate and added to her mystique, although I knew the nuns at my convent school would not approve of her. She had a cat named "Dog" and drove a cute sky blue 180B Datsun with a large yellow rubber ducky imprinted on the front. She was a woman of contradictions and contrasts; sophisticated to her boyfriends and child friendly to her patients, all things to all people. Her attitude was laisse faire and bubbling over with passionate energy. Her games consisted of chasing the male patients in their pyjamas around the hospital until she would catch them. She would thrust that desperate petite body and attempt to hug and lock lips. Her hair would flop around in soft red tufts as she ran. Looking back, I suppose she is in my memory like a young Nicole Kidman. She was a different beautiful to my mother, flirty and carefree rather than warm and traditional. My younger roommate, Ian, enjoyed the game and would cry out in impassioned glee as he was chased, making sure that he always "lost." To be caught and kissed, however, was, in my mind, to lose the game. This was the normal night time routine and afterwards she would read to us. "You're not calling me Boss!" I yelled out when I was caught. For me pretence was not part of the game. "Only GP calls me Boss."

"You're not my boss, darling," she would reply in her deep, phlegmatic voice. Then I would turn away or cover my face with my hands, only to have them smothered in kisses by her lips and be left lying there in a cloud of musk perfume.

Her actions were an imposing of a will over mine and attention I didn't want. In fact, the ultimate defeat. I did not enjoy being told that I stunk and should shower. It was her domain and her resources. I was just a fly caught in her web of whatever it was she was spinning. My secrets and feelings were all that I had and if I was caught and kissed, they would be in the open. For this reason, I thought it was cruel that it was written in the final summary of my time in Stubbs that I had "a dislike of women" and that I displayed "some physical aggressive behaviour towards women usually during rough and tumble." Perhaps I should have presented her with a dozen long stemmed red roses and chocolates before each chasing game, but it was a case of "eyes wide shut."

Miss Raatz's overt chasing and kissing contrasted with my mum and dad, who were not overtly affectionate. Similarly, my school run by Catholic nuns was very conservative when it came to different gender relationships. My early experiences of a sexual nature were finding pornography on boards in the old shed behind the school that the nuns didn't know the students had access to. I felt as if I was exploring a dark cave of sin in the nether reaches of my mind, punctuated by unnatural pinkness, curves and growths I had not seen before. Most of my early experiences of adult romance came from peeking at the adult programs on TV later in the evening, or the family motoring past the town drive-in when they didn't realise what movie was playing. Occasionally, Dad would ask Mum for a "TV kiss." My siblings and I all knew what he meant. The fact that he was given short shrift established in my mind that there was some evil attached to it. It was certainly reinforced by the priest's sermon on a Sunday and even more by the visiting Bishop, who would shake as he told of the unvirtuous young man who died of a heart attack after he had turned away from God. Ironically, the most I learnt about sex was from the extended discussion and lunchtime that the nuns afforded the students on one of his visits to the school.

Several years later, I found country first love was much better than city, especially in the spring after the winter rains. I guess it helped being older and having early puberty. Everything was green, pure, fresh and unadulterated, a bit like me when it came to affairs of the heart. The sweet, natural smell of newly grown or cut spring grass was so tangible and physical. I would leave the monster behind and lie down where he used to play with me, so dead for so long, and swoon. I had never noticed so many of those small bell-shaped flowers before. It had been a very wet winter. The spring growth was driven by the strong September sun that warmed me nicely. This second love experience was different to my first. Of course, it would all end in tears a few weeks later, when I discovered that you actually had to talk to your girlfriend and see her to maintain a relationship. In any case, I remembered Miss Raatz and thought that at least we hung out and went to the movies together.

It was a motley crew that gathered in the hallway ready for our night out. We would all have been wearing jeans and an assortment of what I'm sure would have been garish windcheaters. I suppose the group must have included Rennie, Ian, Roy, and the self-appointed "sex symbols" of the group, Diane and Bruce. I didn't argue with them about this status as I was not entirely sure what a "sex symbol" was. We were to be joined by Miss Raatz and one other nurse. Now I was leaving the nightmare for the evening. I felt sophisticated knowing the older kids were going into the city and I had been invited. Any change to the routine was good. Maybe this place could be fun after all.

Prior to the outing my day had been difficult. I felt down. In fact, it was to be my worst Saturday at the hospital. I had spent most of it in front of the box, with access to the city channels and programmes that I wasn't allowed to watch at home. It got to the point where Skinny Minnie was calling me "square eyes" and parading me in front of others. They teased me and tried to pull my chair back. Perhaps it would have been better if I had gotten up. I could not drag myself away and had been bombarded with what seemed to be, in my current frame of mind, unspeakable terrors, tortures and brutal deaths. I felt like the warriors in Greek mythology that I viewed being tested for their strength, climbing on ropes above canyons of burning fire, most falling eventually into the licking flames. If they survived, they were only to be further tested by cruel scourging. Their pain and panic became mine as I brooded and obsessed. I wondered how human beings could concoct such awful atrocities to inflict on each other. Next came the movie *Lord Jim*, about a man lost in regret and anger, who wanted to be, and was, tortured. He did not fear torture, he just feared death, because if he died he could suffer no more for his perceived sin of leaving the sinking ship of which he was Captain. I likened his directionless journey into the unknown to my own.

We were to go into the city on the train on the Fremantle line. This was to be something new for me. My only experience with trains on the farm had been for commercial purposes. I knew that Dad always ordered carriages to be left at the siding conveniently down the road from the shearing shed to take away the wool clip, which sometimes amounted to a hundred, two hundred kilo bales or so, at the end of every shearing season. Simon, my two older cousins and I, would help Dad and Uncle John load the bales from the back of the truck to where they would remain on the carriages until picked up by the diesel. I found the new style of train to be a lot more satisfying and I enjoyed the ride into the city.

When I stepped out through he hissing train doors I realised I was on the threshold of a whole new world. I was on a date with Miss

Raatz, and I was going to be good. I knew that she loved me because she was always trying to kiss me, even if I did have to compete for her attention. She introduced us to local icons such as the supermarket, "Charlie Carters," which seemed as big as half the shopping hub of Narrogin, and the Hay Street Mall. Busy people rushed around me out into a seemingly dirty and noisy 1975. It was obvious that this was a very different place to my country town and long yearning nights on the farm. I briefly had more interesting problems than facing the monster, and new experiences to explore. In the city there was a lot more of everything. It was a quick look around and then off to the cinema.

The movie theatre in the city was like nothing else I had been to. We had a movie theatre in Narrogin that was in the centre of town. Like the drive-in on the town's outskirts, my parents saw it as a den of iniquity where the poor values of society were enlarged a hundred times on the big screen for all to see. It was in a constant moral battle with the Catholic church that was built on a hill on the opposite side of the community. Certainly, for me, the movie theatre had a sense of mystique, if only for the reason that I had never seen inside it. Sometimes I would wonder if those large double doors really led anywhere. It was a gaping monster, with large brown jaws that would consume all tender, young and unsuspecting morsels who took a step inside.

This theatre was completely different. It was modern and exciting with red neon lights flashing: "HOYTS: Young Frankenstein now playing" invitingly out the front, and there were two cinemas. The corridors we stepped into were long, wide, and lined with streaks of burgundy. Full-sized colour posters of Gene Wilder, Robert Redford and Paul Newman stared back at us with sparkling eyes from the wall, while the crowd cued up for their Saturday night blockbuster tickets and swarmed around the candy bar like bears to honey. The foyer was air-conditioned and serving staff in handsome red skirts or waist coats busied themselves with content looking patrons wearing jeans, flares and the fashions of the day. I had never smelt popcorn before and I awed over this strange new aroma, especially when a box of it and a soft drink were thrust into my hand. What was it about this skinny, mop haired ten-year-old that everybody at the movies loved?

We marched on to the cinema entrance, led by the inimitable Miss Raatz. She handed our tickets to one of the young red suited staff, who for some reason that I couldn't fathom, tore them in half and returned them to us. Upon entering, I immediately noticed the crimson curtains at the front and side of the cinema and boundaries marked off with golden rope. We found our seats in the middle of the theatre. I wasn't sure if I wanted to sit by Miss Raatz or not. In my hesitation, the seats either side of her were quickly taken by Bruce, the "sex symbol," and Ian. *It doesn't matter*, I told myself and took a seat near the end of the row. The seats were luxurious and padded. I felt like a king. I kept my eye on Miss Raatz, while also being fascinated about what would happen next. *Am I really at the movies?* I thought.

In fact, I was not at all dismayed when I found the film was in black and white. An enormous Gene Wilder stared back at me with an ironic grin and a conceited and ignorant laugh. The horror characters reached out their bony fingers from the screen. I sat glued to my seat as I was engulfed in in a sea of large images and sound and enjoyed the humour and suspense. I was fascinated by the enormous pictures, as we had driven past the town drive-in many times while a movie was playing, but had not actually been inside. The sound was a new novelty. It seemed incredibly loud and to come from everywhere at once, although I knew this was not possible. I was totally absorbed for two hours, before, suddenly, it was over too quickly, and it was back to the bad dreams.

I felt like a different person when I stepped outside. The city lights seemed to have grown brighter and a gentle breeze ruffled my hair. I felt like I was in love, but I was confused about my feelings. I knew I had a yearning. I eventually got a word in with Miss Raatz. "Gee, that was great," I said. "When can we do that again?"

"Very soon, I hope," she replied. I was over the moon once again with excitement.

"Cool," I muttered back in awe. In fact, I was so impressed I presented her with my remaining popcorn and burst into one of my favourite 1970's songs. She smiled politely as I sang.

Over the next few weeks, we would go to the pictures on a Saturday night and watch blockbusters such as *Airport '75* and *The Towering Inferno*. Each experience would be better than the last. The patient group would change, but always one of the nurses would be Miss Raatz. Each time I felt her presence. In the years to come the movies would always interest me and make me feel good. I would remember the emotion and excitement juxtaposed against the misery of that time in my life.

On the train home I sat in respectful silence. I had been on a group date with Miss Raatz and thought it had been a success. Well, I had enjoyed myself. She was cuddling with Bruce and Ian. I looked across and saw the joy and triumph in their eyes. I felt a little lonely, but not really surprised at the realisation she could never be mine in any shape or form. I decided that whatever happened, we definitely wouldn't be playing the kissing game tonight.

The Bully: Home 8 (1973)

I ran into him one day at the local pool, some months after I returned from Stubbs. The memory is etched clearly in my mind. I was immediately frightened of him. Not just because he was three years older and scowling. He had not changed, boorish to look at with his stringy shoulder length blonde hair, and as he was naked from the waist up, I saw he was still quite scrawny, with arms and legs like twisted baling twine. I kept eyeing his hands and long fingers that had caused me so much pain. My inner mind noticed his hard outer shell and eight tripod style legs. Arachnid minions ran around at his feet. The spider would never be dead while he was around. In actuality he was tall, with an arrogant expression and sneer of someone who did not consider the world worth his time. He leered down at me, so confident with his total victory. "I hear you had to go away, Kain. I'm really sorry about it," he said and added with a laugh, "game, set and match." Our eyes briefly locked. We both knew his victory had been final. He had broken me.

When I was younger, I would often awake with cramps in my back. The pain was so severe I had dreamt I was breaking apart and death was imminent. I pondered how my spine could spasm and bend like that and not break. I didn't understand, so I would pray, "Oh, God, dear God, make it stop." I researched it, but found the New Testament had no references to Australian spiders or transforming monsters. The pain was in the area of my back where the bully used to hit me.

My back was always sore at primary school. Once older others recognised it was sore, it was targeted. As he approached in the playground I would see the shadow of the monster. He would stop and it would hover over me, blocking out the sunlight, just as in my nightmares. I would walk into his web most days at the start of recess. The more I struggled and confronted the horror in my mind, the more I felt the sticky netting lacerate my skin. Once I was caught a talon would wrap around my back, exposing my kidneys, and allow a painful blow from his horn like proboscis. My teeth would ring from the strike and my body would shake. He would sometimes drool his spittle into my hair. I could only struggle helplessly as one of his furry eight legs would sandpaper it into my skull. It was a small school where there was nowhere to run and nowhere to hide. Everyone knew who was bullying who. I didn't try to avoid him as it was a ritualistic event. I was told I "must take my medicine." Perhaps, somehow, I thought he would be merciful and live out the values of the school iconic Religious Education programme, but he had no compassion. Part of his quest was to mark me as a victim for any other predators. That way I could be wrapped in their webbing and saved for later.

Narrogin was a merciless rural town. I was targeted and assumed helpless, with my flossy blonde hair and baby face. I got red easily after exercise and was noted as being sensitive and academic. He believed age gave him seniority, but on reflection, he was defined by a culture of indifference and ignorance. He wanted a target he could have an impact on. He would call me by my surname as if my belonging to my family was a precursor to final damnation, and he had the say in my pathway in life. I knew he had friends that represented the non-practicing catholicity within the school. He belonged to the school set who believed you didn't need to go to mass to be important. They knew my family were committed Catholics and they were worried they were the ones mentioned in the Sunday sermons: the pack, gang, or mob to stay clear of. They did not often work together, instead preferring the lone wolf approach. I would get a clip over the ear out of the blue as I watched from my favourite warm spot on the bitumen overlooking The Big Boys' Playground, or hear "I've got a guts ache, Kain." I would be punched hard in the stomach and told, "Now you can have one too to go through the rest of the day with." If he couldn't be seen to be big among his tougher older peers, at least he could seem big to those smaller than him.

I remember one terrifying day he grabbed my arm and pulled me viciously into the toilets away from prying eyes. The smell of the toilets still lingers in my nostrils. They were the oldest part of the school, and as it turned out, were close to being demolished and replaced. For now, their interior was a mass of grey render and black slate, broken up by two small cubicles and a grille above the urinal through which leaked a little strangled light and the cries of playing children. He would throw me on the cold concrete floor amongst the dirt and urine and assault me with what he called "the typewriter." Filth would get in my hair and soil my uniform. The floor would be cold and hard. My back would crack while I worried that my mother would see and smell my clothes and wonder what I had been doing. In my mind's eye I saw and felt the monster's minion spiders running over me, sinking their tiny fangs into my unprotected skin. I knew the act was beginning when I would feel large knees pin my much smaller arms. He would sit on my pain wracked body and talk me through it. He tried to make me mute with terror. "You tell anyone about this, Kain, and me and my big mates will have to come after you with my knife and it won't be pretty." A knife! I felt my own warm urine escape and add to the blood on the floor to form a sludgy mess. "I'll start right here," he added with a grim laugh, and he jabbed me in my small throat.

Later on, I realised he did not have a knife, but just the threat was enough to change my life. I knew of knives. I had watched Dad dumbly as he trussed up fat lambs in the wheelbarrow. Suddenly, as if out of nowhere, his sinister long knife appeared, thin and cruelly razor edged after being sharpened many times. He would hack at the jugular, through the wrinkled skin and wool, until the artery gave out and blood would cascade into the barrow and over the ground, first a dribble, then a gush. The final killing act would be delivered with a crack and grind of the bones as the neck was broken and the head would flop lifelessly on the side of the barrow with the sheep's tongue lolling. Incisions would be made on the knee joints and the legs dismembered so that the hide could be sliced off the skin and punched out. Was I nothing but a sheep to the bully? I wondered ridiculously if I would I stink like they do when I was sliced open.

"Fingers on the chest then, Kain," he would say. He would start to happily hum the typewriter tune. "Diddle, diddle, diddle, diddle, dum! Diddle, diddle, diddle, diddle, dum!" His bony fingers would dance across my upper body, poking so hard that I thought they must come out my other side. Each time he reached the end of his tune his long talons would slap a stinging and insulting blow on my face to "return the typewriter carriage." My body was screaming for him to get off me. I was repulsed and squirmed with loathing. He was touching me where normally only my family would, but I was helpless in the wake of his threats and too small to resist. I glimpsed on the wash basins the enormous dated and inexpensive soap bars that the school saved money on by buying at low cost or received as a donation. They were enormous bricks of rough texture that could be taken apart in your hands in great flakes when dry. Their scent of exaggerated perfume was overpowering, the school hoping a strong smell could compensate for the cheapness of the product. I longed for something clean and fresh now, something sanitised or bubble-like to be put between him and me. I needed to wash and scrub my skin raw. I wanted to be home, even if it meant hiding, so the bully could not find and skin me.

"Ding!" A hard slap on the face jolted me back to my senses. "Can you see the light, Kain?" He laughed. "Keep moving towards it. You'll feel good like me. I feel better every time I poke you. In fact, I just can't seem to stop."

Once or twice an older boy came in and laughed, one mockingly gagging at the smell. The bully told me no one would find out, and if they did, they wouldn't care. I knew for certain no teacher would ever find me in there with him. He was creating the pecking order like the chooks I had seen in the coop that would find the weakest chicken and climb on them, pecking and lunging, bedraggling, and exhausting, leaving the victim to wander the yard limping and bereft of feathers.

The end of recess could not come quickly enough. At its conclusion we would line up in the school undercover area in front of our rooms, shortest to tallest, and face the principal. *The*

River Kwai March music would play. Our feet would commence moving on the spot. Our arms would swing at the joints, as if controlled by some unseen puppet master. Out the front, demanding respect, was tiny Sister Bernard with her long ruler at the ready, prepared to deal with any tardy miscreants, fully forgetting the abusive bullies. Peeking out with her glasses and veil just visible under her enormous wide brimmed sun hat, she reminded me of Colonel Saito, the short dictator appraising the prisoners and personnel at his disposal. I glanced sideways half expecting to see a Japanese machine gun nest in the tuckshop, but saw only bored mums and one or two students emerging from the "hot oven" of detention. It seemed to me that working in the field had been just as tormenting. She gave the nod to the teachers to begin the march back to the bridges of education, whatever the cost. The pounding of feet began. It was as if an ordered entrance into our rooms could compensate for playground incidents.

In we marched humming as we went, "Bullshit... and the same to you, bullshit... and the same to you." The monster drew my eyes to the seniors. I rubbed my black eye and I saw the bully and his mates sneering in my direction and making cutthroat gestures as they sang under their breath with the rest of the school: "Bullshit, it's all bullshit, it's all bullshit..."

Country Roads: Away 9 (April 1975)

After a good night out at the movies I was in love with Miss Raatz, but because I was angry with her, I resolved to talk to her as little as possible and certainly not be kissed. To be honest, I felt my relationships were insignificant. It probably wasn't a good thing, I decided, to be unimportant to others in a mental institution. One afternoon in my first full week at the hospital, I decided to go and see GP to ask him for more merchandise to pick me up. I found him sitting with a newspaper in front of his face. "No Clues in Shirley Finn Murder" screamed the bold headline on the front page of *The West Australian*. I didn't know who Shirley Finn was, and to be honest, didn't care, but I wanted some attention. "Who's Shirley Finn?" I demanded and whacked the middle of his newspaper. No response. The next time I was a little louder. "Who's Shirley Finn?" I demanded and whacked the paper again. This time he threw the paper down in disgust.

"Don't do that, Boss, or in future I won't stop Cowan taking you to the room." This statement made the hairs on the back of my neck stand up. I knew he was joking, but it was obvious I had riled him.

"I just wanted some attention," I confessed. "I feel like I'm being ignored and a bit low. Do you think you could give me some merchandise to perk me up?"

He gave me his best stare. "Sorry, Boss, I can't help you with that, but I might be able to let you go home for the long weekend at Easter." My heart missed a beat. Did he say, "Go home?"

Easter was only two weeks away. Somebody had heard my prayer and recognised my suffering. I was too excited to speak. "I mean you'll have to resume here after the break of course," he continued. "I think I'll be able to convince the powers that be to let you go for a while. How have you been sleeping?" He must have known I was restless at night and hadn't yet established a satisfactory sleep pattern.

"Not bad," I fibbed. I was desperate to get home, even if it was only for a long weekend. It was certainly something positive.

"Well, if you're sleeping okay, I think it'll happen. Also, I need to let you know that your parents are coming up tomorrow. They want to bring up some more of your gear and sign paperwork. Make sure you're on your best behaviour."

I felt like a man who was clinging to a cliff top that had been given a rope. "Of course," I replied. I was up for whatever it took

"Oh, and by the way, Shirley Finn is a prostitute, a lady of the night."

"Oh, you mean like a sex symbol?" I questioned nonchalantly, as if I spoke about it every day of my life.

"Yeah, something like that, now will you let me get on with my reading?"

I sat down to watch TV, but I was too excited at the fantastic news. Instead, I walked out the back in the gentle sunlight where some other patients were playing. The hum of bees and the aroma of native shrubs was elating. The banksias were drowsing in the afternoon haze. I began to sing – in my best choir boy voice – a song that an aunt on my Mum's side had taught me. It was called *Feelin' Groovy.*

A million thoughts were racing through my brain. Would my

family accept me? Has anything changed at home? And then the really big one about the family visit. If the door was opening about my leaving, what if Mum and Dad thought I was so unhappy here that I couldn't possibly stay? At last I would be able to tell and show somebody.

***

I felt so good that I decided to have a shower for the first time at the hospital. My anger was subsiding, and I thought Miss Raatz would be pleased. Showering was an independent decision and not something that had to be done. I grabbed my toiletries and change of clothes while I was still feeling brave and headed downstairs to the shower block. Thinking back on my time at Stubbs, I decided that I probably did wash quite often, once the "drought was broken," so to speak, as my room always smelt of soap. I actually enjoyed showering once I got into a routine, but the first time I found daunting. I passed Rennie and Bruce on the way down. They looked at me quizzically. "Where ya' goin'?" Rennie asked curtly.

"To have a shower," I responded brightly. Rennie shared a furtive glance with his mate. He must have been thinking, if this guy was going to have regular showers, then he might not come across as madder than me. Certainly, he wouldn't stink any more.

The bathroom facility was enormous and much bigger than the small family bathroom at home. It was always glistening clean with many shower cubicles, open tiled space, and a large luxurious bath with a separate door, but sometimes I felt anxious in this great big space. It was the same feeling as when I was stuck at the animal sheds doing the chores while dusk was coming. I wasn't sure about all this space being unaccounted for. In any case, I left my clothes on the outside bench and tentatively ran the shower. I washed myself while trying to keep aware of what was happening in the bathroom, in case somebody, or, as an awful fear was prodding me, something, worse might be there. After a few minutes in the shower I heard the door open. Rennie had come in to clean his teeth and Bruce was with him. I considered afterwards that they were the odds they liked, as they were both older and bigger than me. Suddenly, feeling naked – literally and emotionally – I turned the shower off and quickly got out and dried myself. Rennie was dressed in his royal blue dressing gown and his perfectly brushed hair exaggerated his widow's peak. "Flight 747 now leaving from runway three," he boomed. "Next stop is Poofter's Paradise." In panic I looked around quickly for my clothes, but they were nowhere to be seen. Hurriedly, I wrapped the towel around my mid-drift as they came over. "So, you finally did it," Rennie said. "No more stinky poo for you."

"Have you seen my clothes?" I asked. "They were just here on the bench." I looked around the vanities, in the other shower recesses and even the toilet cubicles, all without success. I knew this was not going to end well.

"What do you think you're doing sniffing around the toilets?" Bruce offered. I kept looking and they let me stew for a few more minutes.

"Oh, I'm sure they're floating around somewhere," Rennie commented at last, mostly for Bruce's amusement and then burst into laughter. "Follow us." They led me into the bath recess where the bath was full of water and... *Oh no*, I thought, *surely not*, but on close inspection, yes, those were my clothes I saw floating in it.

"Why are my clothes in the bath, Rennie?" I asked.

"Well, we thought after we pissed on them that they would probably need a wash," he laughed.

"Yeah, that's what you get for messing with our girl. Stay away from her, you hear?" His warning had more than a hint of menace and I could only conclude that he was referring to Miss Raatz. "Next time, it'll be you we piss on."

I couldn't believe his response and felt repulsed and beaten. It seemed I'd gone from one lot of bullies to the next. His expression confirmed he was proud of what he had done. I shuddered at the thought of their bodily fluids on my clothes. They had quite clearly gone beyond the pale. I realised suddenly that I was living with patients whose personal culture carried no empathy or understanding of their effect on others. Either that, or they were plain evil. The mutual diagnosis the other patients had made about Rennie seemed to be confirmed. It worried me that I might be as obnoxious as these guys if I was in hospital with them and might have some of the same repulsive traits. I found it embarrassing, in retrospect, that they both left the hospital before me. "Well, at least you know they don't stink like you," Bruce got out between bouts of laughter. Sometimes I wished Rennie would take off in his plane to Poofter's Paradise and never return. He was one dude that I didn't get on with and I was a bit surprised at Bruce as well, who seemed to be constantly undermining me. Rennie appeared to have suddenly found a friend for nefarious purposes.

I felt the presence of the monster strongly. Perhaps this is what I had been watching for in the bathroom. The monster was here. He had invaded my new space. He now lived in my hospital and could walk through the walls to wherever he wanted to be in my life at any time. "Well, you'd better get them out before they get too wet, stinky boy," Rennie chortled. They left with howls of laughter. As I retrieved my clothes, I reflected that my first bathing experience at Stubbs had not gone well. In some ways my misgivings about it had been justified. I didn't think at the time to tell anyone about the incident. It may not have helped if I had.

***

The day Mum and Dad arrived I was up early to cook the bacon, as was beginning to become a routine. I thought about my conscious plan for them as I did it. I considered that they might even pick up on subtle hints. I mean, wasn't it obvious things weren't going well? Did I need to make it clear? I was working myself up, so I concentrated on what I loved – cooking the bacon. Everyone was very happy to let me do it and it seemed to be appreciated. I loved the sizzle and the aroma. The warm greasy smell would waft through the kitchen and arouse the taste buds and nose. I was "the bacon king." I would cook it in a lot of oil and watch while it crisped up and turned in on itself. "Well done" was my speciality and crispy bacon was in demand. It was easy. Some mornings I would cook fried eggs as well. I loved the neatness of the metal rings that went around them that we didn't have at home. It felt nice to actually not have to be involved in collecting the food before I cooked it.

Mum and Dad arrived later in the day. It was to be just an afternoon visit. I thought I must be insistent that things weren't going well and that I had to go home, but things didn't happen as

I expected. I was waiting out the front in the car park when the familiar station wagon pulled in. I rushed to meet my parents. I was keen to tell them I would be coming home soon. I hoped it would be for good. Mum was dressed nicely and wearing makeup. "How are you my brave little man?" she asked and gave me a hug.

Dad just looked tired and annoyed, as if he was upset at being away from the farm for a day. His expression seemed to contrast with his snappy suit and crisp white shirt. In any event, he said he was pleased to see me and shook my hand after he had got the case with my possessions in and handed it over with a, "Here you go, Paul. This will make things a little easier for you."

I wanted to spill the beans straight away. I thought through my questions. How are the animals? How is the family? Do the students at school miss me? Did you know I was coming home for Easter? What should we do at Easter? I wanted to tell them about Cowan and the room, Rennie, the bullying and isolation and my night out with Miss Raatz. All I could manage was, "Boy am I pleased to see you," and, "I want to come home today," before GP whisked them away to an interview in his office.

Afterwards we went for a drive to the nearby sports oval. I had a kick of the footy with Dad. It was pleasant and a good chance to ask all my questions and catch up on the news. Upon returning, as we were sitting in the foyer waiting for tea, I became anxious as I realised time was running out to get my point across. Couldn't my parents see that I had already been forced to grow up and face my fears? To a ten-year-old a few weeks was a significant time. I wanted to leave. I wanted to leave now. I wanted to go home and be back with my family. I knew my parents could make it happen. It had not really been long since I had seen them, but it felt like an eternity. I wanted my parents to know though, that I wasn't happy about it. The time for small talk was over. "Please don't ever leave me like last time," I suddenly exploded. "How could you abandon me like that? Can't you see how unhappy I am? Do you know how I am treated? Like nothing, like a fly on the wall. They all think I'm insane and laugh at me. Do you know that I spent hours crying on the steps after you left?" I waited for a reply but got none. "Well, do you?" It occurred to me that I was being a little unfair; at least they had taken the trouble to come and see me and perhaps would not come again if I got upset, but I had to take the opportunity to tell my parents while they were here.

Mum stared at me, shocked. "We would never leave you, darling, if it wasn't for the best. Mr Peers says you're doing fine. I don't believe things are as bad as you think. You're making progress and getting better."

"No, I'm not," I was adamant. "I still do repetitions through doorways and tie my shoelaces repeatedly. I hang out by myself at school and am really struggling. How can you know what it's like having to start at a new school? I'm away from my home and family and locked in a hospital with crazy people." I knew I was working myself into a state, but I was feeling more and more powerless.

Dad looked angry and seemed to me to be trying very hard not to give me a clip over the ear. "You don't know how lucky you are, son. You've been given a great opportunity here. Your problem is you're too smart and in too much of a hurry to get everything done." Is that what he called it? A great opportunity? Did he mean crying your lungs out, being placed in a padded cell and being threatened with electric shock treatment?

"Can't you see?" I raised my voice and pointed my index finger at my temple. "They want to fill me full of drugs and zap me, zzzzzzzzzzzzzrrt!" My parents looked at me, speechless with horror.

"Well, um," Mum stammered. I thought she might cry.

"You just don't care, do you? You're down there and I'm up here. They can do what they like with your ten-year-old son."

"I'm sure there's been a misunderstanding," Dad finally said. They seemed immovable. They had put up a force field protecting them from my pain and sheltered inside it. I was left alone outside to fight my own battle with the monster. It seemed I was right where he wanted me.

I didn't feel like escorting my parents down to dinner, but I knew I had to. I no longer believed that I was responsible for anything that would happen. Patients and nurses were filing into the dining room when we arrived. I looked at the menu board. I was disappointed to see that we were having steak and kidney pie. It had been on the menu once before and I hadn't eaten it, preferring instead to fill up on fruit. Getting used to the menu was one of the pitfalls of my new accommodation. I was quite often suspicious of different food. I didn't want my parents to come to dinner and then watch me not eat anything. I loved steak and pies, but I was genuinely put off by the thought of eating kidney. I had seen what it was in its original form when Dad butchered a sheep for the family. Quite often he cut it out and threw it to the dogs.

"What are we having?" Dad asked once I had escorted him and Mum to a table.

"Steak and kidney pie," I replied. I don't know if I looked

sickly, but I certainly felt it. When we had our meals, I began picking through mine trying to identify what was steak and what was kidney. I thought I would eat only the steak, but I couldn't always tell it apart from the small round bits of kidney. I put some food in my mouth, but it wasn't going down well. I drank a little water. I identified more kidney and realised that I had eaten some by mistake. I felt bilious and close to vomiting. I gave up fighting. I had had a hard day and I just let it all go. All the frustration, anger, anxiety and loneliness came out in a fluid rush. It went all over me and all over the table. *How bad was this*? It must have splashed on my parents as well. I had vomited in front of the staff and other patients in the dining room when my parents were here as guests. It had been a chance for me to chaperone them and demonstrate how I had progressed, but it had gone pear shaped. Now my actions would be discussed at length and analysed at staff discussions, where knowing looks about me would be exchanged.

For all my careful planning of conveying my case for coming home, I somehow felt guilty. Had I in fact really intended to vomit? I decided, probably not. Perhaps I was just anxious. A nurse came to help me clean up and Mum and Dad moved back out to the foyer to speak to GP. Surely they were working through the details of my going home. I couldn't possibly stay after this. Once again I was wrong and had lost spectacularly.

Intended or otherwise, I felt as if any progress I had made had been washed away. I think on that night, by hook or by crook, I sentenced myself to a much longer time in hospital. I just hoped that I would still be allowed to go home at Easter.

***

"So, what are you going to Narrogin for?" I asked the well-dressed, middle-aged man I had sat next to on the WA Rail bus on the Saturday morning prior to it beginning its Easter trek into the Great Southern. I was in a good mood and wanted to be sociable. There were double seats available that were not taken, but I liked company and had anticipated that this man would be friendly and appreciate a chat. I had made sure that I had showered and not chewed my fingernails.

"I'm not going to Narrogin. I'm going all the way to Albany," he replied casually. I noticed that he was an earnest fellow and trying hard to be polite.

"Oh," I replied and felt a little embarrassed. I looked around and was disappointed that all these people weren't really going to my home town. I had assumed everybody was, as when GP left me at the East Perth Rail Terminal, he told me it was the bus to Narrogin. Perhaps, in my anxious state and my desire to get home, I expected that everyone wanted to travel there. It struck me that I had tended to become obsessed with my own problems and was reminded abruptly that people had their own life to live.

"Narrogin is one of the stops about halfway actually," my seat mate added. "We're going the long way, round the back, and not down the highway." I wasn't exactly sure about the direction he meant, but I knew I would soon find out. I remember thinking at the time, *why don't we just go straight there the usual way*? My worst fear was that my parents might not bother with picking me up or be unsure about where the bus stop was. Despite this, I just wanted to be on my way. I had heard that Simon had started playing underage footy and was one of the team champions. Perhaps they would just take an interest in him and forget about me.

As we prepared to leave, the sky was overcast and a few drops of rain fell on the windows, but I was warm inside the bus despite some distant rumblings of thunder. I also felt grown up and important. I was going home independently. "I think we might be in for a really big rain," I confided to the middle-aged man.

"Well, it's about time. We could do with it," he replied after a moment's hesitation and looking up from his reading.

I had seen the storm was coming and purchased a long yellow raincoat. I was to nearly always wear it on my regular Saturday morning bus rides over the next few months, even inside the bus on dry days. I was very proud of it, and, for some reason, thought it was sophisticated. I also always wore jeans and a wind cheater as my bus attire, perhaps it was my way of taking on the world, staring it down or making sense of it.

"Okay, all aboard," the portly, grey haired driver said at last. With a tweak of his official peaked hat he lurched us out of the depot. The large burgundy coloured bus turned to face the oncoming storm and the sea of dark black. The clouds were building up and the sun had subsided altogether. I was an eager participant on the journey and kept an enthusiastic look out the window, fascinated about the new route out of the suburbs into the Great Southern. We set a quick pace once we were rolling. The eastern fringe of the city flashed by to give way to semi-rural lots as we drove around the base of the foothills. Before I knew it, we had stopped. It was a place I had never heard of called York. *What's the story*, I thought? *What have we stopped for? Let's get going and keep the show on the road.*

My mind was active. I was excited. I was going home at last, if only for two nights. I had not yet considered the horror I may feel upon being asked to return to Stubbs. All I could think of was getting there. If the bus did that, by any route, it was doing a great job. Every minute was taking me away from Rennie, Cowan and co, and closer to my family and what I knew. I hoped that there was still a family niche for me. I decided that I could play footy too if it got attention from Mum and Dad. I had also been working on my cricket skills. I had perfected an exaggerated long sloping bowling run that reflected the techniques of the fast bowlers of the day, such as Lillee and Thomson in the 74/75 Ashes series. I was looking to try it out on our backyard grass pitch if circumstances allowed.

As the interminable journey continued on, the weather slowly got worse. At some points I felt the bus swaying in the wind. We stopped for lunch in Brookton. A stop, that this time, I was pleased to make. I strolled out importantly through the rain in my yellow oilskin with the other passengers and ordered, what would become my staple Saturday lunch, a tomato sandwich and a cup of tea. As I ate I felt joy and a sense of relief as I watched the rain falling. People would be happy. I hoped somehow it would wash away guilt and anger. Certainly there was a part of me that could spend a long time listening to the rain, smelling its freshness and enjoying the briskness in the air. It made me want to start over again with a clean slate.

After we left Brookton, I could feel my excitement growing as I started to recognise some of the towns and landmarks that we passed. I began to understand the direction the bus was coming from. I knew that soon we would be driving over the steep hills north of Narrogin and be able to catch glimpses of it in its valley. What surprised me when it finally came was that now I could see the storm clearly silhouetted. It was enormous compared to the town and hovering like a black spider against the horizon. It spat thick mucus and long tentacles of grim cloud snaked from its body to the community's furthermost points to enfold it in a web of nature's fury.

As we drove into town it was clear that the long drought had well and truly broken. Thunder cracked and the rain sleeted down. The noise was immense. The farmers would soon be out working the soil and sowing their crops with the earth nourished by life giving rains. On Narrogin's outskirts, water streams flowed together to form torrents on the surface of the paddocks and rushed soothingly over the parched dry earth, often taking the topsoil with it. The bus began to slow as it was caught in large puddles on the streets and visibility became very poor. I had just said goodbye to the man next to me when I spied the family car at the bus stop. They had not forgotten me after all. It was Mum that emerged into the storm to meet me. I was quickly informed that the rest of the family were at the football ground, five minutes away, watching Simon play. I suppose I had been half right as Dad was not there. Dad was an ex-player at the club. I knew he would be in his element. There would be a great deal of excitement also that it was raining so heavily. He had his own rain gauge and was prone to exaggeration. I'm sure he would be looking to brag to his fellow cockies about how many inches of rain he had had. I rushed from the bus. I was home.

If Horses were Wishes: Home 9 (February 1975)

For several years after the bully threatened me with a knife, if he walked anywhere nearby, I would always make sure that my lips were clamped together and locked over so that he could see I had no intention of telling anybody about his beatings. Sometimes, he would pat me on the back and say, "Good boy, Kain," like I was his pet dog. It took some months for me to stop racing home and hiding from my imaginary slaying at his hand, but the nightmares continued for longer.

My relief gushed like Niagara Falls when he and most of his mates graduated from the school, leaving only a few lesser lights to continue the inquisition. Some afternoons I would just collapse on the dilapidated sofa in the rumpus room late in the day and pray Hail Mary's of thanks while my family would wonder what I was doing. It was at about the same time that I entered Grade 5 and was permitted into The Big Boys' Playground myself, but as my sister had mentioned earlier, I wasn't doing so well. It was a time when the monster grew beyond the size of a planet in stature. He had evolved into the galaxy, with his feet near Mars and his head near Neptune. His choice of plaything was the pretty blue planet that he held between scaly green talons, that could be disposed of, or not, at his leisure. I felt his fiery presence on my neck and smelt his acrid fumes. Only I could see what was happening to us all. I was able to catch my visions of him through the swirling fog that came between myself and other people. He would place a claw in front of his mouth, as a warning to be silent about his plans, and remind me of the debt he owed me for my life all those years ago.

It was during the long, hot and dry months of February and March that things came to a head. I was no longer the champion of my dad or my peers. As the burning sun continued to beat down, school was not as easy as I had anticipated it to be when I was older. Expectations were higher and I was called on to do more on the farm. I was not sleeping well and was anxious. I may even have missed school, but I don't recall this. I had become compulsive and despondent. Mum had taken me to a GP to address the problem, although he had done little and suggested that I would "grow out of it." He could not know of the horrors the monster was planning.

The playground, and sometimes the classroom, had become a network of intricate booby traps to be negotiated carefully or be punished brutally by. The Vietnam War was still on. There was a proliferation of soldiers on TV news reports who had not been careful when they had taken their last step on two legs. It was as if I was moving and everyone else was standing still, when in fact the opposite was the case. I became impervious to other students and barely able to participate. I wasn't sure if I was the centre of attention or completely lost in the crowd. My struggle to maintain relationships and simply not care about what people thought must have been obvious. My friends and community were out there somewhere, but I could not locate them through the fog of paranoia and the swirling breeze of terror. I felt ugly, although I was told that wasn't the case, and marginalised when compared to the girl pleasing machoism of my older brother. The dysfunction in my world was a nightmare, yet horrifyingly true. Any barbs that may have come my way were the least of my problems. Each dusty and dry break time at school would be a search for solace, regardless of others; often, repetitions gave me peace, if fleetingly, and this pleased the monster. I saw objects in the mist that no one else saw that needed touching, often, again and again. In the background I could sometimes hear the cries of other students: "What's he doing?"

"Can he hear us?"

"Don't do that, crap face. You're holding up the game," and the ball would be kicked at my back.

"You're meant to be fast. Why don't you run over and get the ball? Move!" Sometimes, I heard them even complaining to Simon.

"Can't you see it?" I would offer weakly under my breath and reach out to the monster to show my audience. I wanted someone to step into my grey world, but no one ever did. In the end I was reliant on Mum to come in some days with my lunch so I could eat it with her in the car.

When my mother arrived with lunch, I knew I had a friend. However, I would hear teasing such as: "Your mummy's here now. She'll protect you. Are you taking your girlfriend flowers? I hope they are the pretty pink ones with soft petals." It was the ultimate insult in a tough country school.

I felt guilty leaving the school, but as I departed the brown gravel and the playground hustle for the family station wagon parked next to the playground, I felt the fog lift a little. I took comfort from knowing that my peers liked my mother. I didn't want to face the truth that I had finally made it to The Big Boys' Playground and now was running away to another fantasy world. I wanted to be a man like my brother and my past heroes, but I could not emulate their feats. It must have been a slightly humiliating experience for my mother, quite apart from the commitment of time and effort. Appearances were a lot in a small town and my parents and family were respected citizens. It was difficult for us all to accept that we were not going well. To the gossips, or anyone who bothered to notice, it could be a sign that the family was falling apart. I hoped I was just another face in the crowd.

On this day in February 1975 Mum was well dressed in her blue dotted blouse and long leg blue slacks. Her makeup disguised the worn expression of a farmer's wife waiting for the rains with a large family to feed. Her French style perfume was a lot different to the unstifled body odour of primary students and her smile a welcome change from the menace of Sister Bernard's thick ruler. The slight pain she let slip, other than her worn expression, was the sadness mixed with determination in her eyes. This was something that only those close to her would notice. Her pain was worse because she was her husband's wife. A man who had upset fate or God and was now being punished. Simply, to my ten-year-old mind, he had riled the monster. The day of the accident in the paddock, it had made a pact with his son. He had been caught in the web due to his carelessness and arrogance. He had over committed himself. He had too much power and land or too many children and now he was being paid out for having his fingers in so many pies.

The smell of food jolted me away from my thoughts and I realised I had been staring at the school's rickety wire fence.

"Nice to see you, darling," Mum said and offered me my sandwich. "How is your day going? I hope you're feeling brave."

"This place sucks, I reckon," I replied as I took a bite. "I want to leave. Do you know they want to perform an exorcism on me?" The film *The Exorcist* had recently visited the drive-in. The posters for it around the town had caught the imagination of some of my peers who thought they could account for and rid me of the monster.

"That's used to get rid of devils, isn't it? I thought only priests could do it? Who wants to do that?" Mum sounded angry. "They'll have me to contend with if they try anything like that. This is a convent institution for heaven's sake. I'll march them right up in front of the school board." She was a big lady, taller than Dad, and played GK in netball. I suddenly wished I hadn't mentioned it. "You just have to be strong. We will get through this together. Remember the poster of the runner on Jenny's wall. 'The race is not always to the fittest, but to those that keep on running.'" I frankly didn't appreciate the reference to my sister.

"I think this war has made everybody more violent," I said. At the time I thought it was a gross generalisation, but Mum was visibly sadder. I realised I had said the wrong thing as she became very quiet and I remembered that she didn't like to talk about the war, especially as it was near its end and any more deaths would be particularly tragic. Two of her younger brothers, Michael and Danny, had been "winners" in the cruel conscription lotto. They were consequently involved in the Australian military effort in Asia. "Are you worried about your brothers?" I offered sympathetically. I thought Mum was going to cry, but she continued to be resolute.

"Yes," she replied. "You have a problem and I have a problem. We can support each other and get through this as a family. Grandma and Grandpa are worried too, of course," she went on. "I spoke to Michael the other day. You know I don't think he was quite right." She added under her breath, "If horses were wishes."

"Beg your pardon," I replied. I had not heard her clearly.

"Then beggars would ride. It's just an old proverb. It means that if you could just wish for things to happen, then even the most destitute of people could have what they wanted." I understood Uncle Michael's plight, as to my way of thinking he would be facing his own monster. Knowing what I do now, I realised Mum must have been referring to the symptoms of post-traumatic stress syndrome. This was a common condition for returning Vietnam vets. Michael was just starting out on his adult life and would need a career after the war. It did not surprise me that my grandparents were worried. It was a visit to them about this time that I realised how proud of their sons they were. They did not want them to go to war, but they were forced to embrace it.

Grandpa O'Connell would use a haunting voice to refer to his sons in the military as "trained killers." His tone was not wholly ironic. The family had been forced to celebrate their conscription, and I found objects of interest at their Bunbury house in the 1970s that established with myself and Simon a fascination and a curiosity about war. The symbolism was overt. We needed to look no further than the lounge room mantelpiece. Taking pride of place was an Australian slouch hat, service medals and a Vietnam War bayonet. It was long, heavy and polished silver so that it glistened in the light. I shivered when I felt the slight notches and wondered about the damage it might do to a man when it was pulled out as well as initially impaling them. Did it really need to be that long? The knives I had seen and knew of had been practical and tools of occupation. I also thought of the bully and his knife threat. I mulled about a job that involved using such a fearsome object in a professional way. At our grandparents' house, we were also introduced to personnel issue items that we experimented with on the farm, such as pannikins, soldier uniforms and belts. Our open paddocks became, for a little while at least, the fields of Vietnam.

Having brothers affected by the war in Vietnam must have been a great weight pulling on the mind of my mother and her family. I often considered the terror that she must have lived through and shared as she followed the war or caught bits of gossip about what was really happening. I knew Michael was an engineer and shuddered as I thought he might be involved in the disarming of enemy explosive traps or working through Vietcong tunnels. News footage showed young Australian troops in dense jungle facing an unseen enemy and struggling with fear and unimagined horrors. Mum must have silently made sense of her worst fears for her brothers. She cared about her family and was close to Grandma. It may not have been a reason for, but it was a distraction and certainly added to, the confusion that I felt. For Mum it distracted attention from the monster. I wondered about the value judgements that she and Dad were having to make.

"Isn't the war close to ending?" I asked Mum. She looked at me blankly, like a small child who knew nothing. I thought it best to change the subject. "It's so hot in that classroom with its wooden floors. I can't concentrate. I wish I could sit by the window and get some breeze."

"It's important that you try your best, Paul. That's what I expect of you, regardless of where you sit or if it's too hot." I knew also that Mum would be praying for me. I looked up at the giant wooden crucifix, just visible across the playground on the external wall of the convent. We talked on for a little while, but all too soon time passed and it was back to school. I kissed my mother on the cheek and told her I would see her at home.

There were still a few minutes left of lunch. I wandered back into the playground. I immediately became the sideshow to the main event of playing sport as I began performing repetitions.

Suddenly, I heard chilling screams of agony. One or two boys came to tell me that Simon was hurt. They thought he had dislocated his knee. I had never heard the cries of someone with a dislocated joint and I was shocked by their intensity and desperation, as I'm sure other students would have been. Greatly concerned, I raced over to where a crowd had gathered by Simon. I watched helplessly as I realised there was little I could do to fix his ailment, or even ease his pain. I knelt by my brother in desperation, tears beginning to well in my eyes. In the crisis I had forgotten my compulsions. "Somebody do something," I pleaded. "Please help, it's my brother." It was to be the first of many knee problems that led to a series of operations on both legs for Simon. In fact, all of my siblings, myself included, experienced something similar as we inherited the Hair family knee curse from our grandmother. One by one it took us. With Simon still screaming and being supported under each shoulder, I walked with him and tried to offer comfort as he was carried up to the sick bay. I seriously wondered what, if anything, could be done for him. His knee had already begun to swell. The kneecap was pulled to the side at a peculiar angle. In the background I heard the bell ring.

The monster would dislocate my life and my uncle's mind in the same way as my brother Simon's knee would dislocate on the football field and once or twice in the playground. The Vietnam War might have been ending, but for me the battle was just beginning.

Tommy: Away 10 (April 1975)

My return to Stubbs after going home for Easter was traumatic. I had to once again leave my family. To make matters worse I was then told that my weekend visits would be restricted to one night only. I decided that it was still worth going home for that single evening to remind me of what life could be like, even if it broke my heart to have to come back the next day. It was like being told that your cancer had cleared, only to find it had come back again. To my mind, I was either well or I wasn't. I reflected that the feeling of euphoria and release was greater than the downside. I would go home regularly on the weekends after Easter, catching the train into the city and then the bus by myself, and return either with my parents or a lift they organised for me.

Life wasn't as dark when I was home, but it was still like aggressive swirling mists at Graylands School. This was where I would find a quiet place to myself and dream about my weekend, away from the nothingness of trying to exist. I desperately needed a friend; someone to drag me kicking and screaming to what was real and substantial. I was thankful that through the swirling mists, Tommy appeared.

I knew him simply by his first name and he told me he was from the North of England. I assumed from the red soccer shirt that he often wore that this was somewhere near Liverpool. I had heard of Liverpool because of the soccer team. As kids we had known the song "Long-Haired Lover from Liverpool" on the farm and thought it a great joke, as to us it had an alternative meaning. To a boy who had grown up watching his father slice the offal out of dead sheep and blood congeal in a pungent puddle below the carcass, it was associated with something completely different. My initial response was to feel very sorry for Tommy if his town was drowning in a sea of blood and offal. In essence, all that really meant to a boy who had never been out of Western Australia was that he "spoke funny" and played soccer. In fact, he was almost impossible to understand at first. You assumed he was giving you the time of day, until you realised you were being called "daft" or "his bloody lordship." He had red hair and a few well-spaced freckles that looked as if they had met in the middle of his face and then spread out because they didn't like each other. With his stub nose, he could look quite fierce when he wanted to. He taught me first-hand about the intensity of the gang culture in England when I told him and a group of his bigger west country lads that they should play the "real" game of Aussie Rules as I waited at the bus stop one Friday afternoon after our preferred sporting sessions. Their motto was "safety in numbers" and I kept my mouth shut after receiving a North England reprimand. I wasn't sure what a "Glasgow Kiss" was, but I didn't really want to find out.

He loved soccer as much as he hated the threat of Aussie Rules. His short and stocky appearance made him well suited to being a soccer "striker," as did his outspoken nature that demanded the ball be passed to him. He lived with other students at the migrant hostel next to the primary school and would join the flood of child immigrants to the school each morning. I thought that, like me, they were travellers, in some ways lost or unwanted, on a journey trying to fit in and we were together for a time to sort things out. I had my own gang from the hospital that would arrive on the bus from the other end of the campus. It was a much smaller group and the constant transitioning of its numbers made it hard to establish common attitudes. By contrast, the migrant students would stick together. It was their culture that dominated in the schoolyard. I learnt that you didn't need to go to England to learn about English culture. In fact, it was as different to The Big Boys' Playground as you could get. Aside from the culture, the school boasted generous and lush green areas. It seemed that their style was in the tradition of the English Bobbies and demanded that I should use the pleasant facilities and play soccer with them at the breaks, if only because they didn't want anything out of the ordinary happening on their "patch." Their unwritten code was different.

I knew that they played soccer because when I arrived at school they asked me, in a friendly way, to come and join with them. I was nothing, if not well built and athletic, and I suppose they thought I could be a handy acquisition, even though I had never really played their game. Tommy wanted me for his team. My thinking was, however, if I'm not going to get involved with my own sport in my own school, then I'm not going to get involved with people I don't know and a sport I had never played. Dad and my uncles had played Aussie Rules and the sport owned my country town. I should have realised I was in a new town now.

I would prefer to go to my quiet spot outside a classroom away from my peers where I would not be embarrassed or anxious. It was a way of starting again. I didn't want people to know my secret if they weren't already aware, although being a regular arrival from a mental health hospital created its own stigma. Maybe somehow that was cool. At least I belonged to a group. I knew what was going on, of course, in the game, because it would be the constant topic of conversation in the classroom. I always knew who was playing on who and how many goals had been scored. My sporting instincts kicked in and I listened. It seemed to be the talk of soccer that got the migrant boys to the next break. I realised that, like me, they were just trying to get through the day. Tommy was particularly insistent that I play with them. Sometimes he would come and talk to me in the classroom about the game and tell me the details of how I could fit in. As the students left the class he would invite and remind me.

In the end, he came over and saw me at recess himself. I was in my usual place when he approached. I wondered if he had been sent by the group. "What are you doing over here?" It wasn't a rhetorical question. He genuinely wanted to know.

"I like it here," I replied. "It's where I hang out."

"Yeah, but that's daft," he got back to me. "You're by yourself and don't do anything or talk to anyone. Who do you think you are going off by yourself like this? You need someone to knock around with instead of crying and repeating stuff over and over where you think no one can see." I felt affronted that someone was having a go at me for just being alone. Didn't he know that I was the victim here? Tommy sounded like it was my fault and the world was a worse place because of my actions. "You could be a regular George Best," he sermonised, but I looked blank. "Although that would make you a Manchester fag," he added under his breath as an afterthought. I guess I was meant to know who George Best was.

"What about Kevin Keegan?" I offered helpfully. "I've

heard of him." Tommy continued, ignoring me. He was winding himself up now. I figured he was upset because he was short and had a go, while I was taller and didn't try.

"You've got a choice you know. Why don't you come and play with us? We'd love to have you and it'll impress the lasses that you sometimes talk to over here. We can be strikers together. You tall, and me fast. You'd be good with headers and all." I politely declined, but as he left, I thought about his offer. It certainly had been insistent, and someone had come over to be friendly at last. Didn't they know about the monster? I found it hard to believe that they just wanted me to play regardless, monster and all, as a new friend and one of the group.

During the next class session, against my wishes, Tommy spread the word that I was coming over for a look, maybe a kick and that I was good. I liked Kevin Keegan, apparently. A boy wearing a Manchester United shirt came up and asked me if I was a forward or a back. "A forward, like Tommy, I suppose," I mumbled. He gave me a knowing look before continuing.

"Well, I'm a mid, so I'll be able to kick it to you. I'm a rotten player, but I give it a go."

"Don't take no notice of 'im," the boy behind me responded, after getting my attention by poking me with a ruler. "He'll only kick it to you if he you give him a couple of quid for the canteen. Bruce is the one to watch out for, that bastard's crash hot."

I had seen Bruce in action. His claim to fame was that, like me, he was a great runner, but unlike me, well respected and king of the schoolyard, as much for his calm demeanour and fairness, as anything else. He was the alpha male of the Year 5 group, the strong silent type who moved like, and had the balance of, a coiled leopard. Tall and strong, he had the reddish hair colouring of Tommy and carried the mantle of athleticism for the class. Even Mr R – who was the school AFL coach as well as the reading teacher – was in on it. "I hear you're going over for a kick of soccer at lunch," he said. Then he added with a thumbs up, "Way to go dude!"

I became a little nervous and uneasy as the time before lunch approached and I thought *What have I been forced into*? I was being set up. I couldn't play soccer and certainly didn't want to become the centre of attention, although a little bit of friendly, positive involvement had been pleasant and unusual. Perhaps it wouldn't hurt just to return some interest. Soccer was an okay game, and not hard to work out. It seemed some of the love for the game of the hostel boys had rubbed off on this Aussie football fanatic.

In the end I was totally undecided about what to do. I had to fight the monster hard to resist walking quickly away out the classroom door as I became anxious after the bell rang. The decision was more or less made for me, as I perceived what seemed a large shadow, or it might have just been a presence.
"Is it true you're good?" It was Bruce, blunt and straight to the point.

"No," I replied, but I was flattered by the attention. "Soccer's not my game." I tried to walk away.

"Well, why don't you come down to the pitch and show what you've got anyway?" I might have been able to say no to Tommy, but Bruce was a different kettle of fish. I got the impression that if he wanted something, it normally happened. Suddenly, Tommy was by my side.

"Come on, mate, I'll walk with you," Tommy said. Turning then to Bruce he added, "He is good and all. He can be a striker in my team." I felt like I had been handcuffed and marched off by the Bobbies as I walked to the pitch surrounded by the soccer gang. I felt uncomfortable and could not ease my anxiety. The group seemed to have expectations of me. I felt like I had something to lose, especially with Bruce being on my case.

Tommy and Bruce were captains. Tommy immediately boosted my confidence by picking me. I stood next to him while the teams sorted themselves out and then tried to walk to the side-line as they went to their positions. "I think I'll just watch for a bit," I offered nervously. I was wearing jeans and wasn't really dressed for active sport. Tommy was aghast and put his face near mine.

"I'm not waiting for bleeding doomsday. I picked you, you sackless article. You'll bleeding well play. Stand on this side and look lively. That's our goal," he said, pointing down the long sloped green to a pair of witch's hats. "Make sure you put something through it, or you'll not be picked again." I wasn't sure exactly what Tommy was saying to me, but it didn't sound like he wanted to be messed with. Bruce's team took their shirts off and the game got under way. Tommy was immediately everywhere, although he was meant to be a striker. He motioned for me to follow him up the field.

I soon realised that it was a game for the disorganised rabble, and I would be struggling to embarrass myself, but after a few minutes hadn't really got involved. "Just chase the sodden ball and kick it," Tommy yelled. He took the legs out from under an opposition player, whose bare torso went sliding across the grass, to leave him with control of the ball. "You're not even gettin' a sweat up, you skiver. Here you go." He sent the ball rifling out of the pack towards me. Suddenly, I was besieged by three bare chested migrant boys who were kicking ferociously at my ankles. I swung my foot wildly at the leather and tried to gain a few yards, but the ball was quickly won over by the opposition. Tommy was breathless and unimpressed. "What are you doing, you great lummox? Are you taking the piss? I passed it to you and all and you just let them have it back."

I was surprised by Tommy's reaction and that I actually felt crestfallen. At least I thought I should get marks for participating. I took a moment to admire the sublime skills of Bruce who hovered over the ground and made the ball disappear from opposition boots like magic. I thought briefly about what Kevin Keegan or even George Best would have done. Tommy came over and put his hand on my shoulder. "Didn't you say you played?" He asked, more sympathetically.

"Actually, I said I didn't," I replied. "I'm more Aussie Rules," and added quietly, "... and can run."

"I thought that about you Aussie Rules fags, no guts," he concluded. Tommy was definitely fishing for a reaction, but considering the present state of play I just went with it. "Perhaps you should go back to tossin' around by yourself outside the Year 7 class."

"Yeah, perhaps I... hey," before I could complete my reply the ball had come back. He grabbed me by the arm and pulled me towards it. In fact, he pulled me through a pack of sweaty, frenzied boys hacking at it. Afterwards the ball was nowhere to be seen, but a player I assumed I had run into was on the ground holding his shoulder.

Tommy screamed with delight. "That's the way, put 'em on

their backside. They'll not come near ya."

Following Tommy's lead, for the rest of lunch I became a human battering ram and even got a few kicks away. If I got the ball, I tried to direct it in his general area. My ankles and shins were killing me, but I guess it had been worth it. As the game finished Tommy offered some praise, even though it had been a draw. "Two all's a good result considering they had Bruce. You did well once you got going. They started getting out of your way. See, I said you were good."

In the afternoon lesson I felt happy, like a battle had been won, both within myself and against the monster. I realised I had enjoyed it and felt more a part of things. Tommy was certainly beaming and wanted to tell everyone about the game I had played in, leaving out the parts where he had abused me or pulled me into other players, of course. I was always keen to participate after that and formed a good striker combination with him. I even kicked a few goals which gave me a thrill and he acknowledged that it was "pretty good for an Aussie Rules dude." It was just a step along the way though, as it wasn't what I was really good at. I wanted to show what I could do. The more I watched him, the surer I became that I could beat Bruce in sprinting. I noticed that he was a bit slow off the mark, whereas I was quick.

It was about three weeks after I had first played soccer that I saw my opportunity. Some Tuesday afternoons were allowed for extra sport time. Now that I was playing soccer I would increasingly look forward to sporting activities. I had this day pencilled in, as it was the day of the class trials to find the qualifiers for the athletics carnival. Tommy had been pestering me about it for a few days. "Are you going to run, Paul?" he enquired.

"I reckon I might," I replied. I didn't let on that I was itching to, and in any case, it was compulsory.

"Well, you won't beat Bruce. He always wins everything."

"Thanks for the confidence, Tommy. You said yourself you thought I was good."

"Sure, but Bruce is a... legend, unbeatable, you know what I mean?"

I remained quietly confident as the classes gathered for the hundred yard dash. Dressed in my sports uniform and with bare feet, I made sure I fitted in with the other Year 5 students. I passed the time fidgeting nervously. I hadn't been doing any training, but I had been getting some sport in. I tried to remember the basics, and the things Dad had taught me. It all seemed so far away and so long ago. I reminded myself who I was representing, where I came from, and what I stood for. I decided it was important who I showed my ability to now. I could do something I was good at, even if I was entirely by myself. It was hardly the Olympics, but it was important to me. In my imagination, I could see the tall grandstands and the crowd calling.

"Year 5 boys you're up next, so let's move it," Mr R boomed at last in his deeply authoritative voice. Ten apprehensive boys shuffled into their lanes. I was in a middle lane, which was promising. Tommy was next to me. We both looked across at Bruce at the far end, who was relaxed and smooth as always. He seemed focused. I realised then that this was going to be something special. This was my chance to make an impact. I took some deep breaths and enjoyed the aroma of the freshly cut grass. I was comforted by it being soft beneath my feet. I felt strong and knew my legs would hurl me down the track. "Don't let me down now," I told them under my breath. I concentrated on my start as I knew it was important.

"On your marks!" came Mr R's call and the group walked up to the line. Suddenly it didn't seem so light-hearted any more. A hush of expectation was in the air. "Get set!" The gun was raised. I waited for it to gush with noise and smoke. As I went into my starting stance I squatted low and stared at the finishing tape that seemed so far away. I reflected that the course was unfamiliar, and it ran slightly downhill. Bang! We were off and I surged.

I got a fast start and my legs felt good and strong. *I must get to the front* I thought to myself. Half the boys had given up in the first forty yards. I felt Tommy slipping away and dug in harder, flicking sweat as I ran. I realised I could do it at the halfway stage. I was in front and knew that if I kept going I would be the new Year 5 champion boy. Bruce must have been second. I felt, rather than saw, his presence gaining and mowing me down with his sleek leopard movements. It was neck and neck, but he had left his run too late, as I had reckoned. I had done it. I took the tape a yard in front. There was no fanfare or trophy presentation. I don't think I even got a ribbon, but the school had seen the win and it was important to me. I had beaten Bruce the legend. In my own mind, at least, I was trying and going in the right direction. He came over to shake my hand and was smiling, content to pass over the mantle of fastest boy in the class, if only for a short time. I felt at last that I fitted in, even though there were a few confused looks among the students, but Miss Noske silenced them and extended a smile in my direction. Tommy came over to me and uttered breathlessly, "You are fast and all. You beat Bruce. Why didn't ya do that on the soccer pitch?" I was taking some deep breaths, trying to get some air back in my lungs, when the pretty blonde migrant girl who I remembered had referred to ants as "unts" came to over to me. I knew her name was Rita.

"Hi, Rita," I greeted.

"Hi, Paul, you are so brave. I liked that you won." Before I could stop her she reached up and kissed me on the cheek. I was completely taken aback, and felt myself blushing. "Oh, you've gone bright red an all," she giggled. "You're my new 'ero, just like Kevin Keegan."

As I walked back to class I thought about my mother. She would never know Tommy's name, but would have been thankful to him and his Pommie mates that asked – no insisted – that a boy from country Western Australia, an outsider in a new environment, just like them, should be their friend.

Voodoo: Home 11 (March 1975)

The monster would often remind me of the deal in March 1975 as the aridity and heat continued on. I saw him in strange places: at school, on the bus, watching television and in my normal routine. I saw him every day in bullies and became frustrated by his presence, as repetitions and isolation would not satisfy him. Some days the tension would consume my sweating and writhing body. My anger would bubble over. I would hit a blameless student, for what I thought was just beating me to collect a ball. In actuality, perhaps I was unhappy they were accepted, and I was not. It was the monster that would not let it rain. I tried countering his power by lying down and letting rosaries flow through my hands, and the Catholic prayer of supplication to Mother Mary, *The Memorare*, flow from my mouth: "Remember, O most glorious and blessed Virgin Mary, that never was it known that anyone who employed your help or sought your intercession was left unaided…" Surely the Virgin Mary could not ignore the prayer of a young Catholic altar boy, so I felt some confidence in the prayer's conclusion: "…despise not my petitions, but in your clemency graciously hear and answer them. Amen."

Often, my anger would not be sated after I had completed a prayer. I would need to pray it again and again. It did not feel right. I lamented my lack of faith. At the Catholic church every Sunday, the parish priest would preach from the ornate lofted pulpit at a congregation housed beyond the fenced off altar, telling of the need to have faith and how you could overcome difficulties and be safe if the Lord was with you. As an impatient child with a literal faith, I expected an immediate response from my prayers of meditation to mend the ways of my world. I would realise years later that the Lord was probably somehow carrying myself and the family, but the monster would not let me detect his presence.

I had more control over imaginary games of sport I played by myself in the backyard in which I made up characters and teams. I could always win by hitting sixes and scoring goals at crucial times. I took to walking up and down the driveway some evenings, drawing naval battles with a stick on the hard white sand that would imprint my naval strategy for many rain-free days on the black moist dirt underneath. I knew my victories were hollow fantasies. I would look in the mirror, see myself growing and wonder why I was not winning – someone somewhere was – but it was not me. I wasn't happy at school and work was not being completed. I would turn the pages of my maths book at the same rate as the best students, but not understand what I had done or ask questions that showed I did not understand. My teacher, Sr. Bernard, saw positive traits in other students and held them up as examples. I was jealous of them.

Mum grew more desperate. Some days she saw my plight in the playground with her own eyes and realised I couldn't stand being away from her and had developed a dependence. She could not be everywhere. My father told me that I must "get a grip" and "stand on my own two feet," but he still encouraged me to complete chores around the house that would help him out. He seemed surprised that a son of his was not able to act on his advice and establish a positive direction in his life.

Almost as a last resort, Mum thought she would try an appointment for me at a different GP. This was a situation that I was not comfortable with. I preferred the regular family doctor who I had been to on several occasions. I would not tell him much, just have a brief chat, wait for Mum to have a longer one, then we could go home. The status quo would be maintained. I suppose he knew what would happen if he recommended further action. Ironically, in the end, it was not the family doctor that referred me to Stubbs, but the young up and comer.

On the day of the appointment that led to my sentencing myself, everything at the new surgery was different. The polished silver "Dr Staer" plaque was as unfamiliar as the location close to town. The entrance, through palm shrouds and imitation tropical greenery, was like a path to a jungle hideaway. It was a particularly humid and stifling March afternoon. I swatted away mosquitos and garden bugs that assailed me as I walked. I felt shattered after a difficult day at school. My jaw tensed with a sense of foreboding as soon as we entered the waiting room and reported to the faceless receptionist. I was determined that this new doctor would not discover the secret of the monster. The deal had been made. It was all I had and the last card I could play. We sat down and I stared at the mandatory large stack of adult reading material on the waiting room desk. A glimmering colourful comic caught my attention among the *Reader's Digests* and *Women's Weeklys* and beckoned me. I chose it gleefully. A few minutes later, Mum's name was called. I was upset when she was asked into the doctor's suite by herself and left me alone in this strange place with people, in my paranoia, I felt were looking at me. They seemed old, tired and listless. They stared as if I was a tasty morsel, now defenceless. She wasn't the one that was ill after all. Didn't she think I would be anxious? I had to fight back the desire to enter the doctor's room uninvited.

Mum seemed to have settled into a long chat with the doctor. I tried to get engaged in the comic I had chosen. I noticed it was not a *Disney*, *Archie*, *Phantom*, or even a war comic. *Voodoo World* screamed the title. I had heard of voodoo, and it did not seem appropriate content for a comic. It was something else entirely. From my avid reading, I knew a belief of voodoo was to have a lasting spiritual identity that survived the death of the body. I thought of my deal with the monster and felt bile rise in my throat and butterflies begin to move in my stomach. Was I meant to be dead? Thoughts of black magic, ceremonial rituals and animal sacrifice entered my young head. As I opened the comic semi-naked indigenous adults with painted on skeletons and theatrical face makeup stared back at me, shaking skulls on sticks. I was reminded of the long-horned cattle skulls, worn white by the hot sun, that I would walk past and wonder about when I was collecting mushrooms on the farm. Sometimes I would pick them up and display them on the top of fence posts. I realised I was not collecting mushrooms now and this was something much more sinister. Why would you be so concerned with skulls from dead animals? The natives carried long machete knives and wore top hats and animal teeth necklaces. I felt my hand trembling in fear and wanted to put the comic down and ask the receptionist if I could enter the doctor's room. In utter panic, I realised I could not speak. It was as if my lips were sewn together. I saw in the comic an image of a voodoo cloth doll. I was the doll. Could it be that stitches were being inserted in my mouth? I felt powerless under the spell. The walls wrapped me in their darkness. I was alone. I was magnetised to the comic. I realised I had no choice but to read.

The story it told in panels was set in impoverished South America. It was about a domineering father, a peasant farmer called Matias, and his twelve year old badly scarred son, Diego. Diego would not follow the community rites. I saw in their village something of my present plight. It was in drought and an air of desperation hung in the air as stock died. Rituals for rain and sustenance performed by witch doctors were ineffective and farmers would wander bare paddocks, searching for fodder for stock. Many were starving. The father's wife had died. All he had was his son, his chickens, and his desperate beliefs.

To his dismay, the son turned to the solace of the new Catholic mission priest, Father Alfredo. Diego would sneak out at night to attend church. One night he was followed by Matias, who having caught him, threw him at the feet of voodoo elders to impose punishment. After spiritual cleansing using chicken's blood, he was taken by his father to the coop where he was locked in. The coop was dark. He could not see the stars. He was fearful and disorientated. In their panic the tens of chickens, that he thought of as friends, saw him as a predator and became flying projectiles. The claws of the chickens scratched at his deformed face. They drew blood that attracted other chickens and he became a victim to be pecked unmercifully to death. He knelt and prayed that his mind and body would survive the ordeal and that Father Alfredo would come and raise the power of the cross against the voodoo curse.

Somewhere in the story, I became Diego, and felt his helplessness and confusion. I heard and felt the screeching chickens and recognised the horror of his tortured expression. I had experienced the blur of flying birds like lead spheres, their eyes shining in the dark as they made their frenzied attacks. Like Alfredo, I wanted to wake from my dream, but did not know how to and could not. My jaw tightened and I felt as if I was sweating inside my head and the back of my neck to lubricate the dry patchwork of my brain. I became desperate to protect the precious eyes. "Please," I prayed like Alfredo. "Let me not be blinded. Do not take my sight." The starving chickens had nothing to eat and now were eating me. I was to become a carcass, like those buried behind the farm shed that Matias would find in the morning. In a moment's relief I saw the glint of the crucifix as the coop door opened. It was Father Alfredo. His opening of the door let in a torrent of thick, warm blood. I saw it now. Like Alfredo, I needed to be cleansed. The witch doctor had placed my doll in a sink of chicken's blood to drown me.

The sea of blood began to rise around me in the darkness. Father Alfredo seemed to be calling out something calming, but blood was lapping at my feet and my toes began to feel wet and sticky. The chickens were caught in the blood and became grotesque – flapping, flicking blood and drowning each other in their confusion, as they could no longer fly. The blood clung to my bare legs and rose to my knees. I tried to stand on the roosts to escape the deluge, only to have my head bang on the wooden beams. I knew it would be over once the blood was above my neck. *I mustn't die here*, I thought, not in this stinking cesspool of faeces, filth and disease.

Suddenly, I was no longer in the comic. I floundered in my reality back in the waiting room. Desks, chairs and magazines were floating at my waist. Everywhere there was blood, smeared, fluid, suffocating and sickly. The other patients seemed to be outside, clawing at the windows with deformed faces and whispering indecipherable words. They were trying to get back in, appearing concerned, but the barriers between us were too great. They could not help. I soon forgot them.

I looked down at my vanishing torso with disbelief. I vaguely wondered where my mother was and what she would think. I did not have time to ponder who was responsible or how it had got to this. I was floating now. My feet could not touch the floor. I was close enough to the ceiling to hold the light for stability. I tried to get my bearings and glimpsed the door to the doctor's room. My mother was in there. She could help. I plunged into the thick crimson tide and reached for the door just as my head began to bob against the ceiling. A wave of nausea swept over me as I went under for the first time. It seemed the witch doctor would have his way. I could not see under the mire. Coming up, I snatched a final breath of air before the room was fully consumed by liquid. I heard a rhythmic thudding noise and could not find its source until I realised it was my desperate hands banging on the doctor's door in a final act of defiance. My lungs were screaming for oxygen and my sole focus was on getting through that door. *This is it*! I thought – except it wasn't. A little air squeezed through a small crack in the door and then light, as the door gave way. I fell through the open doorway, breathless and distressed. The blood had gone. I was wet only from my tears and perspiration. My grey school uniform clung to my skin. My blonde curls fell loosely on my cheeks as I waited on all fours, like one of the farm kelpie's puppies. My mother looked shocked when she spoke. "What are you doing here, Paul? You should be in the waiting room."

"I was desperate to see you," I stuttered, half crying. "There was this comic and voodoo..." I looked up at the tall and young Doctor Staer for the first time. Had I lost control of reality? Where I was? What I should be doing? From the reaction of my mother and the doctor there was little doubt in their minds.

"I think, Mrs Kain," he said, "that this confirms my diagnosis. He is clearly not functioning. I will sign the referral to a psychiatrist now." With that, he took out an elaborately long pen. With a flourish he scribbled on a sheet he handed to Mum. His features glowed with contentment at his victory.

"What... what diagnosis?" I asked from my position at the foot of the door. No one heard me. I could not have my say. He had not even spoken to me. It was as if my lips were sewn together.

The New Doctor: Away 11 (July 1975)

I settled into a more positive time at Graylands school after making some friends. I learnt the way of things, such as playing soccer at lunch times and Aussie Rules during organised sport. I improved my maths and English, but the months at Stubbs passed slowly. I adopted a regular routine that I became familiar with, including going to the farm for one night at weekends and then being distressed upon having to return to the hospital the next day. I always wanted to stay home. I found it best to throw myself into the daily routine: breakfast, school, afternoon tea and pills, play time or sport training, homework, television and being chased sometimes at night by Miss Raatz. Ian had left some time ago, so there was less competition. There was the occasional movie such as *The Towering Inferno*, excursion or visitor. I tried hard to do the right thing by not running away, even though others did. Shirley Finn's murderer was not found, and Gough Whitlam continued as Prime Minister. The Vietnam War officially concluded.

The small picture was fine, but the big picture wasn't. The patients at Stubbs were always changing. Eventually I was the only "survivor" of the first movie night. Rennie, Roy, Bruce, Diane and others had all moved on, along with several of my mates, and some who had stayed only a few days. This was confusing as I considered many of them more disturbed than myself. I felt like the "old hand" when new patients arrived and

I took delight in asking them what their problem was, showing them around, or speculating with the established patients on whether they would cry or not on their first night. *Did my parents actually want me home? Had I been forgotten?* I was in no man's land and caught between two worlds. My OCD had dropped off dramatically after the first three weeks in hospital. I only very occasionally found myself completing repetitions. Some staff were transient, but I got to know many, such as Skinny Minnie, Fat Cat and Miss Raatz, very well, to the point that sometimes I would wake up the night nurses in the morning to get the day started.

I didn't ever get to like Cowan, but thankfully his shortcomings were recognised. He was around less and less. I tried to not take an interest in the padded room section of the hospital, but occasionally heard noises when I was playing table tennis close by. GP didn't ever run short of merchandise. Somehow it made me walk taller. I continued to be upset about my ongoing "sentence." One cool afternoon towards the end of July, I saw him chatting to Mr Williams, a senior nurse. In my paranoia I thought they were plotting against me. In actuality, it was more likely that I would be forgotten about rather than plotted against. In any case, I was a little agitated and annoyed by their arrogance when I asked GP, "Have I been here the longest of the current patients?"

"You've been here longer than any patient before," he replied. I was surprised that he was so forthright. He called his mate over. "Mr Williams, would you agree that Mr Kain has been at this hospital longer than anyone previously?"
I found Mr Williams to be not very supportive or comforting. He looked like Larry from *The Three Stooges*, with his slender

appearance, bald head and unruly mess of hair around his ears. He was always a little detached when it came to my issues, wanting the harder option for me. I felt relieved he was not my assigned nurse and felt sorry for any patient he was allocated to. I remember he had given me a lift back from the city to Stubbs one day and despite my best efforts at conversation, had not said a word. He had just been mechanical in his driving habit of one hand on the steering wheel and one hand on the gear stick while blaspheming at other motorists.

"I would have to check my dates," he replied. It was as if he was required to confirm coordinates for the next atomic bomb blast in the Pacific. "It does sound about right though."

"Doesn't that make you a failure then, GP, if you are the nurse responsible?" I said cheekily.

"Of course not," GP had hardly blinked an eyelid at my professional criticism. "It's just the way things have worked out." I'm sure I saw Williams smirking.

"Well, why have I been here so long?" I pre-empted his reply by adding a possible answer in case I heard something that I didn't want to. "Is it because I'm from the country?"

"That's part of it," and to my great surprise he added, "perhaps, we can organise a decent trial period at home for you." I just about fell over. I had been trying so hard for so long and was now to have my delayed reward.

"There's a new doctor coming in tomorrow. I'll arrange for you to have a chat to him after school and we'll see if we can get something happening." I was speechless and had to sit down. "That's shut him up, Mr Williams," GP concluded with a laugh.

The next day I could barely function at school. I wondered who this new doctor was and what I had to say to get released from

Stubbs. As I sat there wondering, the clock seemed to be moving in slow motion. I considered the options from all angles as I tried to do my schoolwork and not be preoccupied when talking to people. The constant rain falling outside created a rhythm of monotony in my disengaged mind as I watched the water scurry off the roof to form puddles in the garden outside the Year 5 classroom. Once, Miss Noske caught me in a distracted moment and spoke sharply. "You've made so much progress, Paul, but I really am disappointed you're not on task today." Even Tommy noticed and told me in no uncertain terms when we were playing soccer that I should look lively or get off "his pitch." I didn't mention that I might be gone for good. I didn't want to build my hopes up as I had been let down too many times before. I felt I couldn't discuss the situation with anybody and more distant from people than I normally did.

It was still the monster's world and he kept me quiet. I contemplated telling the new doctor about the monster, even though it may not like it and consider our deal broken. What would the consequences be? It was getting to the stage where I was desperate to leave and would do and say anything I thought that people wanted to hear. Ultimately, I decided to just try and tell the truth. I figured I must have progressed even though I would hear the occasional comment behind my back, "He's still doing it."

When I finally stepped into the visiting psychiatrist's office that afternoon, I didn't get what I was expecting. This professional was young and friendly, with a pleasant manner and warm smile. I immediately felt at ease and that I had a mate. He wasn't even dressed formally, preferring a woollen jumper to a tie. His long dark locks were slicked back and must have bordered on a length unsuitable for his profession. His eyes were a green hazel like mine, and welcoming. His body language was non-judgemental, and his skin seemed devoid of the aging and wear that I had regularly come across in my experiences with staff in the last few months.

He bade me sit down. When he opened his mouth I could see his white and well-kept teeth. My game plan and considered approach just went out the window. He was different to Dr Robinson. We seemed to be on a similar wavelength. We made our introductions and he started asking me questions. I had the sudden inclination to tell him everything from beginning to end. It felt strange that I had this urge and I divulged personal information that I wouldn't have shared before, even with GP. It was a case of telling a new friend secrets that you would never tell people that you knew and cared about. I decided that it was a fresh start, and that my story had happened to somebody else. I had simply been an observer. His positive attitude was established right at the beginning with an earnest tone. "I'd just like to say, Paul, before we start, that I've looked at your records and know what you've been through. To me though, you're a blank slate and I'm coming into this interview with no preconceived ideas or expectations. You should just tell me how you see it." I thought that the interview was going well and I nodded in response. "How long have you been here?"

"Five months," I replied. "It's a record, apparently. I think they've forgotten about me."

He gave a little cough and continued on. "Now, why were you sent here?"

"Because I used to repeat stuff, you know, do things over

again."

He paused to make a note. "Now can you elaborate on that or give me an example?"

"I would take a long time to brush my teeth," I finally replied. "I would feel as if they were never clean enough. Also, I would do things like repeatedly putting on shoes and socks or keep walking through doorways. Sometimes, I would have to touch things many times before I could move on." I realised I was revealing information that I would not normally release without a struggle with the monster, or that would embarrass me.

He nodded to show he understood. "That must have made it hard to do schoolwork." I considered for a moment if that was a statement or a question before replying.

"It was actually harder to do work on the farm. It hadn't rained and things were difficult and seemed more important."

"So, you think farm chores were more important than schoolwork?"

"Definitely! I had responsibilities on the farm and needed to get the animals fed before homework. They needed me and would die otherwise."

"Did it worry you that other people would see your behaviour as odd?"

"Not at first, because it made me feel good. Then I thought it would make people feel sorry for me, but it didn't, of course. I think I just frightened them." I was surprising myself with my eloquence and the manner in which my ideas were making sense.

"And how did you feel?"

"Extremely frustrated and angry. Sometimes, I just wanted to hit someone. It was like everybody had an advantage over me and they liked it that way."

"Do you blame anyone for this? Yourself, your family,

people at school perhaps?"

There was a long pause until I blurted out with grim determination, "He won't like it, but I need to tell you that I blame the monster."

"Can you describe this monster to me?"

So, I described the monster for him. I told how and when I had first seen its enormous, armoured arachnid body and made a deal for my life as a young boy. I mentioned the spider minions that ran at its feet in homage, and its long tusks. I continued on: "Drools of saliva drip from its cavernous, razor teeth filled mouth. It sneers at me using the many eyes on its forehead. It is me it wants. I simply have no choice but to do its bidding. It does not show mercy or rest whether I'm in the city or the country."

I told him how it was probably watching us now and I knew for a fact that its talons were grinding inside my stomach and protesting my confession. I explained that it held the world between two of its talons and would press gently to check the effects. "It drains your decisions and your life and leaves behind a dry husk," I explained. "It has the power to hate and create hatred," I added. "It can separate good relationships and make a person feel as if there is no one out there but themselves. Other people become silhouettes or shadows in the mist. You think you have slipped off the end of the world." As he listened, the new doctor accepted my story. He made it sound as if everybody had their own monster and it was the most natural thing in the world. My relief was palatable. It was as if a pus-filled boil hidden under the skin of my body had been popped and the toxins were running in streams down my chest and legs.

"Now, looking at Dr Robinson's notes, you told him that you

yourself were the monster. Is that true?"

I felt a sense of horror. It was absolutely the secret that I did not like people knowing. "Yes, I did say that. I was treated like I was a monster, a young monster, as in that film we saw."

"Do you mean *Young Frankenstein*?"

"Yes, that's the one. Actually, I think there's a monster in everybody."

"What do you think was the worst thing about your condition?"

He was using the past tense and that was a relief. I was moving forward. "The stigma was the worst. In the end, people think you are psychotic, even when you are not. You can't brush crumbs off yourself, scratch a spot, or even use dental floss without someone giving you a funny look. Often, it's the people close to you that jump to conclusions. I suppose it was my own fault they thought that. I just needed someone to believe in me." I added, "I think GP believes in me, sort of anyway."

"Thank you, Paul," the doctor replied. "Well, we've almost finished now. Can you tell me what you've learnt from this sorry state of affairs?"

"I think it's made me stronger than most people and more able to cope. You can recognise mental illness and you know what it doesn't like. Overcoming anxiety gives you confidence in yourself that you can get through what the world throws up. GP calls it resilience. You know like people who overcome an addiction. I've beaten it, haven't I? What are the odds?" He sighed, perhaps he didn't really think I had. "People will never acknowledge it because they've tried so hard for so long to put me down and it would mean that they were wrong. What I think about is if it couldn't be beaten. What if I couldn't get any help?" I concluded and waited for his reply.

He surveyed me for a moment before answering. "Folks have a lot of courage in this world and get help from family and friends. In your case, children should be able to have a decent childhood and that's what we're about here."

"Thank you for listening and I'm grateful for everybody's help," I replied. I would always remember his next words.

"Of course, I'll pass that on. You know I can see the monster too, Paul. As you say, everyone has one."

The weight of lead on my back that I had carried for so long had been taken off by a young friendly doctor that had just been listening without preconceptions. "Why don't you take it with you back to Narrogin? You both can stay a little longer and we'll see how it works out." I stared at him for a full five seconds before my hands began to shake.

"Are you okay, Paul? Let me help you." I began to tremble uncontrollably. The doctor stood up to assist me. I felt my arms moving without me telling them to and as my legs started to give way I took deep breaths and stumbled to the window. I saw a weak rainbow peeking through from behind the grey July weather. It reminded me of the pictures of Christ's power that I so often saw in the primary religious education books, with sunlight glistening through a gap in the clouds. In that moment, I saw Heaven. So, I was to be released for a trial and go home, was I? I didn't realise at the time what a disaster that was going to be.

What's Sauce for the Goose: Home 12 (July 1975)

When I returned home the crops were sprouting and they decorated the furrowed wheatbelt paddocks with fresh, healthy growth. Ewes with new born lambs grazed contentedly on thick winter pasture that splashed generously over the rolling hills. The horror of the long dry stretch had all been forgotten by everybody but the most affected and cynical. Seeing the beauty of the winter wonderland on the bus trip into school, I understood why you might be upset if it didn't rain. I supposed though Mother Nature needed to let the seasons play out. The farm and animals had survived. I had also survived, if only just.

The winter chill was in the air. I hoped I would not get an icy response from my peers as I huddled with them under the veranda in my barely adequate thin school jumper. It felt like the wind was blowing through me and I noted that it had been a little warmer in Perth. Fat raindrops spat and hissed from a dark sky and beat enthusiastically on the corrugated iron roof. I had not needed the man on the radio to tell me that there was an enormous storm coming. It was my first time back at school in Narrogin, only a few days after my appointment with the new doctor. This was going to be the confirmation of my progress. I didn't want to mess it up. I had the opportunity to be permanently home.
There was a momentary hush as tiny Sister Bernard swept past us and into the large, doubled door classroom; it had used to be a

meeting hall, to prepare the day's lessons. She was dressed, as always, in her white habit with a blue edge and long veil. Around her neck was the iconic crucifix of her mission order. I feared she would be involved in any reporting back to the hospital. She had little respect for the power and pomp of the state and believed she was only answerable to a higher authority. Her reputation proceeded her and it had obviously not dulled during my time away. Fear of her thick ruler and lashing tongue had ensured a sense of menace and trepidation when she was present. She had, to quote her own words, "brought bigger fish than us to their knees" and would deal swiftly with any anarchists under her care. I conceded an ironic brief twinge of longing for Miss Noske, but that class was now a long way away and would be going on without me.

I felt like I was just one of the old group that had started in Year 1 at the school, but somehow, I was also different. A regular, but also an outsider and unknown quantity. It appeared I was clothed in a cloak of mystery. I had grown, but so it seemed, had everyone else. A few of my old friends spoke to me, but no one was saying much on this cold Monday morning. I had caught up with some of my peers on my weekend visits. Ken, who had sent me a much appreciated gift, a picture book of the famous tale of *The Three Musketeers* by Alexandre Dumas that I read avidly while I was at hospital, was the friendliest. That was very much like Ken, who was the class citizen and the leader among the group in many ways. He was not intimidating physically. He was pencil thin and bore a similarity to Mr Williams, except for a full head of black hair. Instead, he applied pressure academically. It was always he who led the class on the "Star Chart." It was as if it had been designed just for him to demonstrate his success and be held up as a role model of school achievement. Dwayne was an old mate who was also there, as was Damien, who had taken over as the class athlete, and who I considered difficult opposition. I knew he received coaching on top of his boundless natural ability and strength.

We filed into class. I was allocated a seat next to Dwayne. That was fine as I liked him. His dad coached the school football team and was a prominent member of the government rail office which administered the network around which the town functioned. He was a heavy boy, and big framed. He was smart like Ken, but with a much more cavalier attitude towards authority. He nodded his freckled face towards me as we sat down. We had gotten into a little mischief together from time to time as we both chatted, until it dawned on me that he was chatting and succeeding, and I was chatting and not. He relied on charm and an earnest expression to respond to the directions of teachers rather than abject obedience. "Good to see you back," he offered. "We missed you."

"Likewise," I responded and took out my spelling book. It was "Year 5: Take Two," all be it many months later. I was determined to make a go of it. I flexed my palms with determination.

Everything was going well until just before lunch. I had been concentrating hard all morning, making sure I listened to Sister Bernard, but I was very excited on my first day back and let my guard down. I got carried away with the mood of the room and a little light-hearted banter as the old networks started appearing. The focus was on me as a novelty. I was not normally the class clown. Afterwards, I wondered how I could let it happen and be silly enough to put drawing pins on Dwayne's chair when he got up to ask a question, but I soon regretted it. Perhaps I was angry or upset, or just plain naughty. It happened in a split second and was a crime of opportunity. I spied the loose pins on the cork board and placed them upright on the polished pine as I saw him coming back. He sat down with an "oomph" before shooting back up again. Bullseye! Maybe I felt I could get away with it since it was my orientation time, or perhaps I was testing the boundaries. I was accustomed to teachers taking it easy on me. The idea was to keep it quiet as an in-house joke, but Dwayne made sure everybody knew about it. He was standing up when he called out and rubbed the sore spot. "Hey, who put these drawing pins on my chair?" I knew I was in trouble. It could not be ignored now as the class looked up. I imagined Colonel Saito coming out of the CO's hut to take down the disturbance in the prison camp. In reality, I saw Sister Bernard's intense eyes look up from behind her large square glasses. She tightened her grip on her thick ruler. The room went silent.

"Who has placed drawing pins on Dwayne Reidy's chair?" She questioned with a threatening tone in her Irish drawl. There was no immediate response before her stare settled on the obvious culprit sitting next to him—me. "Paul Kain, stand up." Beads of perspiration gathered on my forehead despite the cool day. I knew I was for it. "Did you put the drawing pins on Dwayne's chair?" I was to receive no support from Dwayne who looked at me accusingly. I knew they had me cold.

"Now you're for it, psycho boy," Dwayne whispered from behind his raised desktop. "Enjoy the pain."

"I... I..." was all I could stammer. I wanted to be safe back in my old classroom.

"Not so brave now are we, Paul Kain?" Sister Bernard asked

me a rhetorical question. "Has the cat got your tongue? Come out here." I walked slowly to the front of the theatre audience that was the class waiting for the performance to begin. I eyed off the ruler, that seemed, in my paranoia, to be increasing in width and flexing with anticipation. She had identified her easy kill. We locked eyes and I realised that I had grown taller than her.

"What have you got to say for yourself?"

"I... I'm sorry," was all I could manage. My guilt was ascertained. The sentence could now be imposed. Sister Bernard used her power to go into judicial mode.

"Were you carrying out an experiment in how much pain you could inflict?"

"No, I just saw the pins on the board and..." I knew whatever I said would not avert the punishment.

"Pain is a fascinating thing," she went on slowly, "and quite underestimated. It can manipulate people, Paul Kain. It could even manipulate you." She was enjoying herself now. "I'm afraid for you that what is sauce for the goose is sauce for the gander and the punishment must fit the crime." I wondered if she meant the ancient form of tribal punishment of "an eye for an eye."

"Now hold out your hands. You must be punished by God for your sinfulness." I thought I might get away with a beating on the open palm, but I wasn't so lucky. "Turn them over," she commanded with a little sneer of vengeance. It was obvious that Dwayne was one of her favourites. She cut me with a searing blow across the knuckles, hard wood on hard bone and pain exploded in my brain. I was just getting my breath back when the second blow landed on the other hand and the exploding pain was renewed. I knew it was personal, by delivering punishment in front of the class it could be nothing else. She spoke again when I pulled my hands away. "Keep your hands out, Paul. Don't you want to be a real man, like your father?"

I had been strapped by Dad, two or three times, as had Simon. It was not unusual for boys in our peer group. He felt it was a punishment he was entitled to give because it's what other fathers did, and their sons had turned out "okay." The occasional event would be ceremonial and sometimes involved more than one son, in order to be "fair." He would notify me beforehand. At the appointed time I would wait and tremble while he would take off his belt and find a quiet spot at the side of the house, before launching a series of stinging blows on my backside. In some ways it was a ceremony of manhood, but always frightening. I was often surprised by the vicious blows as Dad threw himself into it. It seemed as if he was working off his frustrations. It was such a contrast to his gentle stroking of my head at bedtime. He would stop at his discretion when I had been, in his estimation, suitably humbled. It was painful and degrading, but mostly private and always over quickly. The beating by Sister Bernard was something else again.

She gritted her teeth and prepared for a third blow. She hesitated briefly as she knew I would be expecting it. It was glancing, but the fourth caught the bone and I thought I heard a crack. I reasoned in my addled mind how she was justifying this to herself: "Anarchists in the classroom just can't be accepted. God would not accept them." She began circling me like a prize fighter and walked around to hit my head from behind where I could not see the blow coming. A sharp end of the ruler caught my ear lobe. It began to drip blood.

"You can't frighten me, Mr Kain. Don't think you can just walk back into my class from your lunatic asylum and disrupt the apple cart. You have the devil in you." I was determined that she would not make me cry, especially on my first day back and in front of my peers. As if reading my thoughts, she delivered two more sharp raps to my knuckles that were now by my sides. She began to flay randomly at my body. A heavy strike caught me on the shoulder and then I felt my nose come apart and warm blood stream. Red drops spattered the varnished classroom floor.

"Your nose will never be quite straight now, Mr Kain, will it?" She spoke smugly under her breath and looked me in the eye, adjusting her glasses. I tasted salt in my mouth as the tears began to well. She had won and broken my spirit. I sobbed with anger and pain that seemed to wash away everything I had worked towards, all the positive energy, treatment and hope. My body was stinging and aching. I was utterly humiliated. Other students must have been simply glad it was not them.

"I think you have endured your penance. Now resume your seat and do not sin again." Shattered and breathless I turned away, but her lust had not yet been sated. I was standing with my lips trembling when she called me back for more. The monster that had been dormant in me began to move and stretch. I felt sharp talons start to unfurl and prod and pinch in my intestines and a heavy presence on my shoulders. A long sinewy arachnid leg wrapped around my ankle and pulled me backward, its metal like hair brushing against my bare legs. It threw me at the feet of where Sister Bernard should have been. My facade of pretentiousness cracked open. The monster roared with full voice to display its razor teeth and stood on two legs like a human. The skeletal head cracked against the ceiling as it rose, and I thought it must surely break it open. Could the other students see it? Did they know what their teacher had become? When I looked up, it was to confront the monster. It was angry with me and would have its vengeance. Its many eyes were glaring. It was red in the face. Its minions had become other students in the class and its mouth watered with saliva. I thought it was going to end me. In the talon of one leg, it held the thick ruler and blows began to rain down on my forehead, mouth, and stomach. My knuckles were no longer the only target. It struck me on the shins and the knee cap.

Once, when I was a little younger, I had been feeding the chooks and upon closing the chicken coop hastily, the heavy wooden strut resting against the shed door had fallen across my leg and knocked on the knee cap. It was my introduction to acute pain. I writhed on the ground not believing a person could hurt so much. I did not have time or chance to call out to God. For a few moments I empathised with those tortured or forgotten. I always remembered the experience when meditating on the crucifix and Christ's passion during *The Stations of the Cross* ceremonies at Easter. Thankfully, it soon passed, and I did not remember the exact pain, only that it was the most agonising event that could occur. It was there now that the monster targeted. Other students must have seen me cowering and one or two were whimpering or turning white.

To my eternal thanks the heavy ruler finally broke after contacting the top of my skull. Dazed, I limped for the door. I heard an authoritative voice in the background telling me to leave the classroom and wait in the cold outside. I opened the large double doors to see the heavy drops and the grey sky. The great storm was blowing spray on to the veranda. Its bitterness numbed my senses as I contemplated walking the six miles home. I was caught between two difficult situations: more abuse or back to the hospital. It might have been the cold, but I shuddered at the thought of "the room" with Cowan, where I was sure they would send me – for extra mind-altering drugs or electric shock therapy. It would be like I was the new boy all over again. I recognised at last that at least I would not be maimed, or worse. It hadn't taken me long to realise I wasn't wanted at my old school. I set forth out into the rain with my jumper over my hair. I would have to tend my wounds later and hope that my determination would overcome the pain from my battered body. Silently, I offered my suffering for the holy souls in purgatory and reflected on what I had done.

I could not see far in front of me in the rain and mist. I knew the way by rote, but I was not aware of other people that seemed to be like blurs in the distance, indistinct inside houses or cars. They were people I could not touch or communicate with. I felt totally alone with my thoughts and anxieties. If they could see me, they did not seem concerned. I was a foolhardy person from another sphere, pushing on into the rain without an umbrella or coat. Soon even the limited traffic fell away. I was on the outskirts of town. Totally sodden and shivering, I sheltered briefly under the cemetery pergola and listened to my hacking cough. I had suffered from previous chest ailments such as bronchitis and noticed that my phlegm was thickening and changing colour. I looked down the hill at what lay before me. The scheme water pipeline stretched into the valley in a straight silver line next to the bitumen of Williams Road. At the apex of the hill, I knew, was the gate to the town reservoir. I made this my immediate goal and set off again, ducking out of sight if I saw a vehicle pass.

In all, it took me about four hours to walk home in the torrential rain. I turned left at the golf course down Cooramining Road, past the agricultural college and over the railway line. Once I was on the gravel my ordeal was close to ending. I kept an eye out for the school bus, as it was getting to late afternoon. I knew that when I got to the house there would be the other problem of having to face my parents and telling them the events of the day. They would be crestfallen, and there would be an enquiry into my truanting. I hoped I would not get another beating from my father. I thought I would have to win favour by completing chores before I saw them. It would also give me an excuse while I mustered up the courage.

It was after four p.m. when I finally staggered into the home yard. It was still raining. The school bus had not yet arrived. Even though shelter and food were close, I delayed my confession by walking around the top of the house to the animal pens and began the evening chores. It was about then that I heard the commotion of Mum arriving back, having picked up Simon, Jenny and young Nicholas from the bus. I was collecting the eggs and paused momentarily. I heard movement and banging in the truck shed. I realised Dad was working in there. I felt my scalp prickle. He must have heard me, or at least seen the commotion among the chickens. I hid inside the coop and a few moments later Dad appeared, a stealthy silhouette in the narrow doorway. To my horror, he was holding the shotgun to his shoulder. I could see the long barrel reflecting off the fading light through the holes in the tin walls. It was being pointed directly at me. There was no way out, and it was difficult to see in the dark. With a sharp "click," I heard it being cocked. He must have thought I was a fox. Surely he wouldn't shoot his own son. I saw his finger tighten on the trigger. This was one fox that would never attack chickens again. It was all I could do to fling my arms up.

"Don't shoot, Dad, it's me!" In panic, he immediately lowered the gun.

"My God, Pauly, is that you? I thought you were a fox. What the hell are you doing?" He helped me out of the chicken coop and across to the truck shed. He took in my battered and soaked appearance and deep hacking cough. The phlegm landed in globules on the dirt floor. "Here, take this," Dad said and handed me his handkerchief.

"Thanks," I croaked. Coughing into the fresh handkerchief, I saw the tell-tale red spots of blood, stark on the white creases. It was as if I was coughing up my iniquity.

"Pneumonia," Dad offered. It was a chest condition similar to the one that his sister Margaret had died of at thirteen, all those years ago. For a few seconds Dad left me and was somewhere else in his own mind before he spoke. "Let's get you somewhere warm and find out what the hell is going on."

Mum and Jenny looked very surprised when Dad and I stepped out of the pouring rain and into the range warmed farmhouse kitchen. Jenny ran to me to give me a hug and burst into tears.
"It was so terrible you're running away from school. There was a rumour that you'd been involved in a hit and run."

"Well, as you can see, Jen, I'm alive," I coughed.
I glanced at my forlorn mother. She was holding baby Daniel on her hip while preparing food for his siblings. Water dripped from her furrowed brow as she held me in a look I could not decipher.

"Oh, Paul, not again," was all she said. She put down the baby so she could get a towel to dry my hair.

The Voices of Youth

Oh, how attitudes have changed since 1975. Sometimes I think to myself "if only." If only attitudes towards children could be different. If only young people could be taken more seriously. Today, if you are a young person and you are reading this, you are so much more listened to. Perhaps I was a trailblazer before my time. Maybe my suffering left a legacy that meant that other ten-year-olds didn't, certainly not ones from the regional areas anyway. Today, in Western Australia, we have many organisations such as Headspace, Kids Helpline and Youth Focus, offering support for young people. As a young person, you can be comforted that we have resources like the Telethon Kids Institute, with researchers such as psychologist Dr Monique Robinson, where treatment for mental disorders have moved on from measuring heads and locking away the patient. Her belief, in an article written in 2018, highlighted that it's important to take signs of anxiety in children seriously, and help them early on. To quote:

"Often we say to our kids 'don't worry about that' but when there is a clinical problem, it is about understanding this is a problem that exceeds the worries we might experience." Her advice to adults: "Acknowledge it is real and it is serious."

In 2006, a Commissioner for Children and Young People was established in Perth by the state government, with the purpose of (as quoted by their website) "…to make a commitment to the young people and children of WA that they would live in a state where they were heard, valued, healthy and safe." Perhaps though it is more than that. The current commissioner, Colin Pettit, wrote an article for "The West Australian" newspaper in 2018 with the title "Vulnerable children have dreams we can make come true. To quote from that article: "This is an issue that every West Australian should care about." It goes on to ask the question, "Do we adequately resource the services and support that vulnerable children need?" It is recognised that vulnerability is about family. "Support services and interventions that do not address a child's home, school and community environments as a whole are unlikely to be effective."

Furthermore, he suggests that the problem was being explicitly addressed by inviting international, national and WA leaders to challenge how to best address the significant issues faced by vulnerable children in WA. It's encouraging his aim is to explore new approaches that may better help to intervene and break the cycle of disadvantage. To quote:
"Through the consultations done by my office, many of our most vulnerable children and young people have clearly outlined their hopes and ambitions for a positive future and the support they need to achieve this."
Who is vulnerable? All children can be vulnerable and anxiety about certain things is normal, but preventing further anxiety is the challenge for adults. What about, to quote Monique Robinson: "…excessive fears and worries. It might be about specific things (phobias such as the fear of spiders or a fear of the dark) or generalised across life. This worry or fear is not able to be effectively controlled by the child." Children might be vulnerable because of their location, race, bullying, family

situation or outside circumstances beyond their control such as drug use.

In this chapter, I will not be ignoring young people's ideas, but listen to their opinions, ambitions and hopes for the future. Society does not want them just to overcome anxiety, it wants them to have their dreams come true. The following extracts come from a report on the website of the WA Commissioner for Children and Young People titled "Speaking out about mental health: The views of WA children and young people," in which more than seven hundred children and young people aged between seven and twenty three years shared their views with the commissioner about what mental health means to them. If you are a young person, here are the types of things you have to say:

"Know that we understand the feeling of stress and need help to deal with this." Boy, 14

"Oh, this is a little kid. What's he going to know… he doesn't know anything." Boy, 12

"The doctors should listen more; they just make notes and don't tell me anything." Young person

"Telling someone who has an eating disorder that they have not yet lost enough weight to be seen by an ED clinic is BAAAAAAAD!" Girl, 17

"Being teased by the nurses because of my nature and the circumstances of my being sent there did not improve my mental health." Female, 20

"I believe young people aren't educated enough about positive coping methods." Girl, 16

"Healthy minds have the ability to do... anything." Boy, 11

"Where contact wasn't made for a number of weeks, I felt left out and forgotten." Young person

"I get talked to a lot but not included." Young person

"I think that children of all ages should be cared for more than anything. In our life, kids are our first priority." Undisclosed

"Some people think that because we're kids or younger that we don't understand the feelings of stress, but every kid or teenager understands the feeling. The people who treat us like we're too little to understand should stop it and maybe that might stop most of the complications with people or teenagers or kids." Undisclosed

"Talk more to kids. Ask them about their day. Listen." Young person.

"I keep fit and active. This means I'm getting exercise, having fun, and staying away from sad and lonely thoughts." Girl, 12

"Getting enough sleep helps me... because if I don't get enough, I get angry and won't listen to anyone." Boy, 12

"Eating healthy food is good because you get plenty of energy to keep fit." Boy, 12

"Stay away from drugs and alcohol." Girl, 14

"I would encourage people to eat the right foods and to play sports and have enough sleep." Girl, 10

"One way to keep yourself happy is to relax and enjoy your hobbies." Girl, 11

"I keep myself mentally active and healthy by going for a relaxing and refreshing walk down the beach. It lets my mind go at ease." Girl, 12

"When you're celebrating... occasions you're celebrating life, and life is a wonderful thing." Girl, 11

"Be proud of who you are." Boy, 12

"Create goals so that when you achieve them you feel happy." Boy, 10

"Feel good about yourself, it doesn't matter what you look like because everyone is different." Boy, 10

"Friends and family play an important role in staying mentally healthy. They support, encourage and are someone to talk to, and most of all, they are people who love and care for you. So that's why you keep your friends and family close." Girl, 10

"Celebrate the small things in life, because each small thing can build up to be a huge thing that will make you consider that today is the best day of your life." Girl, 16

"Drugs, boredom and peer pressure, they kind of go together." Male, 19

"Try to get more youth centres – football or baseball – one in every suburb – keep kids out of trouble." Young person

"Unhappy means to me that people are not getting enough care in their life from their parents or family members… if children are sad, they think we don't love them and that can cause harm to the child, and when I felt that my Dad and my mother didn't want me, I felt very sad and lonely, but also if I had thought that they hated me so much I would have hurt myself quite a lot." Undisclosed

"Spending time with family and friends is very important because it keeps you happy (especially friends). It is important to keep your family and friends close." Girl, 11

"Because we don't have the opportunity to mix and socialise with lots of people, we actually need events for young people more." Girl, 13

"I put my hand up for all sorts of things at school – looking after the younger students, cooking at camp, being in the school play, if you help out with community projects, you keep yourself active out of school time." Girl, 13

"I would encourage all children and young people to share their stories, share their experiences of a mental health issue they have encountered in life... it's like creating a community possibly online or somewhere you can go to." Girl, 16

"Getting stuff off my chest just makes me feel amazing, especially when they know what I'm talking about, or they can relate a little through their own experiences or how they dealt [sic] with it from an outsider looking [in]." Girl, 17

"I would go to someone else who has the same problem... my friends understood most because they're younger. They're easier to talk to. It helps to share your problems with other kids who are going through the same problems." Girl, 15

"Education about mental health problems is key. It's important to make young people realise that there's no shame in seeking out a psychologist or counsellor to deal with their problems, and that's a far better idea than self-medicating with drugs and alcohol." Male, 18

"More preventative mental health care [is needed]. A lot of times schools and workplaces are not willing to start helping children with their mental health issues until it is actually a big serious problem." Girl, 17

"We should help young people in self-discovery to know that it's okay to share stories with school mates, not keep it a secret that we go through stuff. Empower [young people] that it's okay to talk about it – have school curriculum on topics like self-care, challenges of teens, even at primary school. Help us to empathise and have compassion for each other rather than compare one's situation to another and judge." Boy, 17

"People need to understand that bullying affects you 'cos you believe what everyone is saying about you, and you start acting like what they say." Boy, 14

"I feel sad when my friends don't play with me and say mean words about me." Girl, 7

"Sometimes when I have lots of things to do... I get very stressed. To stop this, my mum tries to help me make a list of everything I need to do and when. This helps me prioritise things and breaks them down into easier chunks." Girl, 11

"In the future schools need to teach children how to accept their peers as they are. Teenagers kill themselves every day because their peers break them by not accepting their differences." Young person

"I was bullied at school for looking, talking, walking, and acting like a gay male. Obviously, this didn't encourage me to come out." Young person

The comment by Colin Pettit, addressing adults and parents, concluding his article mentioned previously in *The West Australian* is apt: "The question is whether or not we are prepared to listen and respond."

The Room: Away 11 (August 1975)

GP had told me that the room would be used to confront my greatest fears, but what I finally saw now was not as I had imagined. At the back of my mind, I had visualised it as a stone walled dungeon containing a medieval torture rack, thumbscrews, and such like. I had ignited the fears of other patients if they asked me if I heard the cries from the ground floor after lights out or felt the cool breezes that would waft through the corridors near the room for no apparent reason. Certainly, I knew there had been patients that had lost their vitality and seemed badly affected, sometimes after only a few days at the hospital. They were not like me and at mealtimes they would ignore your questions and stare blankly with vacant watery eyes, before often leaving the hospital and never be seen there again. Our imaginations would be active with terror when filling gaps in our knowledge about the unknown. The padded room was not unknown. I had seen it first-hand, hadn't I? Sometimes, other patients would ask me about it as if I was the village keeper of memories that needed to be passed down. I would enlighten them about the smell and the sense of helplessness and imprisonment associated with it. Cowan told me that it had been kept for what he ironically called "special occasions." I wondered if this was a "special occasion."

The room I saw, was in reality, more like a glorified woodwork room, but it was dark, dingy, and musty due to a lack of ventilation. I felt myself perspiring in its airless warmth. The only lights for the large room were two naked low-wattage bulbs hanging from cords slung over uncovered beams. The lighting added to the room's sense of mystery, as it appeared to have no end, stretching off into the ether. Tools and other sharpened objects with grim silhouettes hung on ordered wall hooks and I speculated about their possible uses other than for woodwork. I stared through the doorway, only peeking long enough to catch a first impression and the dank smell. I could not move.

I felt, rather than saw, GP behind me, motioning me to go in, but my feet were stuck fast. I knew inside was my worst nightmare. It was the home of the monster and his minions. It surely would be foolhardy to enter. Was Sister Bernard hiding behind a bench with a thick new ruler, waiting for me? Had the bully sharpened his knife for slicing? Was he even now noticing my shadow in the doorway? The stigma and mythology associated with the room, even in the short time I had been at the hospital, created a sense of awe and sheer and utter terror. I knew if I entered it would be for the ultimate battle. I thought I heard Cowan's voice in the background. I tried to turn and flee. A long arachnid feeler grasped me by the ankle and tried to pull me into its lair. "Bring it on," the monster seemed to be saying. I knew it would try and crush me for ignoring and underestimating it. Only a few days ago I had been home and expecting to stay there, luxuriating in the belief that all was behind me; now I was facing my worst nightmare of my own making. Was I fated to be here? Could I really have changed anything, or were all roads destined to meet at this point? I cursed at the circumstances and series of events that had led to this showdown. I definitely had not "played my cards right," to coin a phrase by GP. As my feet stuck fast to the threshold, I thought over the happenings of the last few days.

***

After a prescription of antibiotics and a couple of days in bed, it was back to the hospital. No one seemed surprised to see me. Most thought I had just been away for a long weekend. I fitted in seamlessly. I even got my old room, halfway up the hallway looking over the lawn terrace. The hospital still had the same smell of over cooked food and disinfectant. The beating by Sister Bernard had done little to ease my anxiety, especially, as to the best of my knowledge, she was never held accountable for it. Life went on pretty much for everyone as before, except me. There wasn't a series of clandestine meetings to discuss my misfortune, that I was aware of the implications of, and I'm sure my peers at St Matthew's would have rationalised the situation by saying, "Oh, he's returned to hospital," and got on with things.

Miss Raatz said she missed me. When I said that I had to come back because I couldn't live without her, a bald face lie, she gave me a hug and called me her "handsome hospital man." The trial had been a disaster of mega-proportions and now I was frantic about my normal life slipping away and no one really noticing or caring. The common perception surely would be "I got what I deserved." I had tried everything. I knew under reasonable circumstances I would not blow my chance again, but was forced to face the irony that I had actually run away when I had been home, even though it had been under duress. At least it had helped my OCD. You don't really think about performing repetitions when you are running through a storm with a broken nose. Getting somewhere warm and breathing properly were a superior way of making yourself feel better. Instead, it was a struggle for survival of a different kind.

I realised that the only one who could change things for the better was myself, but the monster had returned. I felt his presence. GP was incredulous when I told him about the drawing pins, the beating by Sister Bernard and the running away from school. He gave me extra pills and said that Dad had suggested that he put some concrete in them so I would "harden up." I think he suspected I may be on the point of conceding defeat to the monster.

It was a relief to be back in Miss Noske's class, but when I told Tommy my adventures in Narrogin, he thought it was a great joke. "Go on, did a little old nun beat the crap out of a great brute like you and break your snoz?" He took my head between his hands and stared at my face to check if my nose was straight. Like a surgeon examining his patient, he ran his finger over the ridge of my proboscis.

"Well, what do you think, Doctor Tommy?" I asked.
"It might be a little off, but I've seen worse," he replied.
It seemed now that I had a broken nose, like Simon, who had injured his playing AFL in Narrogin after a heavy physical clash and was forced to wear a guard the next time he played.

"She was the principal, wasn't she?" Tommy affirmed. "They're meant to look after you, aren't they?"

"Also, she had a big ruler," I replied. Tommy looked blank at that. I'm sure he was trying to think of a soccer comparison and failing miserably. "It was a bit like falling out with the school sheriff," I added for Tommy's edification, as even though he was no stranger to violence, he seemed amazed that a teacher would take to a student with a ruler in front of the class. We very rarely saw our school principal and he certainly didn't come into class and cane us in front of other students. He was an officious, but gentle man. I couldn't imagine him caning anybody.

"Sounds like the wild west," was Tommy's closest analogy. He then proceeded to tell me about soccer violence he had seen in Scotland. "There were a few broken noses there and all. You would see them sometimes on the streets of Glasgow and in other places too."

"Like in Belfast," I noted. Now the Vietnam War had finished, the British conflict with the IRA had been dominating the newspapers. "The Irish know how to give it out, including to their own."

So, I went back to playing soccer on the green slopes at recess time and tried to throw myself into my club AFL football for a week or two, where I was always well supported and liked. One day we enjoyed the thrill of playing on the league ground. I noticed there was an "O'Connell Stand." I wondered if it had been named after someone related to Mum's extensive family. When I was doing something I really enjoyed I felt free from my compulsive terrors, until ultimately, I always had to face them during everyday events.

After I had been back at Stubbs for three or four nights I confronted the monster in a dream. He had been poking and agitating me during the day and when I lay down at night I felt the debilitating agony of cramps around my kidneys where the bully had punched me so often. I had had enough and stood up to him for the first time. My fate was in my own hands. I wanted to be home and away from prying questions about why I was still at the hospital. I wanted to go to sleep every night to the hum of bleating sheep and awake to the lowing of cattle and not face the trauma of returning to Perth. What could he do to me that was so bad? I searched my consciousness for my innermost strength. If he could not stop me searching, then I was no longer his. I discovered he could only do what I let him. I trembled before his enormity as I resisted him in my dream, on the grassy hill next to the rusting windmill where we had first met, while he salivated and intimidated with lunging talons and snapping razor teeth and sent out his tiny minions to hiss and gloat, urging me to join them or die. Terrified as I was, he could not touch me while I was strong. I ordered him to get out of my life. As the battle reached its zenith, I woke up coughing phlegm and blood. My pillow was stained. The night staff came into my room and sat me down while they remade my bed. I knew they would pass on that I wasn't sleeping well and was waking in the night, restless and anxious. I tried to tell them that it was all okay and things were different now. Surely, I couldn't be going backwards.

GP also seemed to recognise the symptoms of my intense struggle with the monster and asked me if he had been bothering me. Perhaps I had been completing repetitions without thinking. He himself seemed agitated and appeared to be adopting a "now or never" mentality. He may have been under pressure from his superiors. He was not used to unmet patient objectives. I guessed too that Dr Robinson, who must have seen it all, probably didn't come across many teachers like Sister Bernard to complicate his treatment programmes. I inferred they figured it had gone on for long enough and they needed something to happen to conclude their treatment. Well, it certainly was about to.

The Spider's Lair: Away 12 (August 1975)

So here I was in the doorway of "the room," like a prisoner, dragged away from my evening activities, with GP behind me, urging me to go in. He had actually given me an ultimatum first and had taken out the long key to the padded cell to indicate what might happen if I gave him any trouble. Was GP, my mentor and friend, threatening me? Had he reached the end of his tether? Perhaps treatments such as behaviour therapy, support group and medication had failed, and it had come to this. I could tell by the creased brow and the intense stare that he meant the choice. He was a little sheepish too that he had been reduced to the cruel simplicity of Cowan and the less experienced nurses. He, now, was celebrating his own "special occasion." For the first time I felt the steel trap of the state. Like a powerful, but flexible band, it was rigid, controlling and systematic, sucking the oxygen from the room and seemingly torching my lungs. It had no beginning and no end, but each time I breathed it tightened its grip. GP was its enforcer. "I can't breathe," I gasped in futility. "Do you get off on this?"

"Come on, Boss, let's get to work. It's all set up," he replied. "I'm afraid it's this, or the last resort is electroconvulsive therapy. Do you really want to be strapped to a table with electrodes on your temples?"

I turned around to look at him. Perhaps the bully, Sister Bernard, Rennie, Cowan and one or two others would have their laugh after all. "You wouldn't do that to me, GP, would you?" I asked through gritted teeth. "I reckon we're mates."

"Yes, we get along and I like you," he replied. "But at the end of the day, you're my patient and I must make hard decisions on your treatment."

The monster had been pulling at my leg. I felt torn. I had my nightmare in front of me and GP behind me, threatening to change who, and even what, I was. I made the only decision I could and challenged the monster for the sake of my family and friends, and the quality person that I believed I had become. They needed me to be a hero. One thing was for sure, I would face it completely alone.

I entered the swirling mists of the room and I lost sight of the monster in the darkness. I saw what GP meant by the room being "set up." Thin pine offcuts were gripped tightly vertical in vices, with what appeared to be names on sheets of paper like "Mum," "Dad," "teachers," "Dr Robinson" and "Miss Raatz." I thought to myself that this was seriously weird. I saw the monster then, sneering, inhuman and impassive. I felt ashamed that GP was witnessing this and it would be in his report. I didn't think I could take much more.

I gulped as he went to the tool rack and selected a large wooden mallet. It got weirder when he handed it to me. I could see what was coming. "This is your mother," he said, and pointed to the name next to the wood in the vice. "You hate her for her dominance of your life. She has it easy because of her beauty. Destroy her!" It was a curt instruction. Was this some sick joke?

"Why?" I asked. "That's silly, I love my mother. I can't do anything to her by crunching her representation with a mallet." For the first time I noticed the warm prickles on my skull. To me it was not rational and made no sense. I knew the monster would not like this, but with GP in my face, I felt the pressure of the state that could not be escaped. I lifted the heavy mallet. It smashed home with a surprisingly satisfying craaacccck! It reminded me of the noise that Dad made when he split a sheep's skull to get at the brains. Like porcelain my mother had been broken and was helpless before my flailing mallet. A victim of my own hand, she had not resisted. I stared aghast, but felt oddly liberated. Where was sanity? This was for mad people to do, not me. How could this help anything?

"Well done," GP said looking pleased. I moved on to the next vice, laden with off cuts ripe for the picking. "This is Miss Raatz," he spoke authoritatively and pointed at a filled vice. "She takes away your dignity and cheats on you. Smash her!"

"I like Miss Raatz," I replied feebly. "She takes me to the movies." I envisioned her flowing red hair and sweet cherry lips in front of me.

"Well, she doesn't love you. Now's your chance. Kill her!" Reluctantly, I attacked Miss Raatz and brought the hammer down, fearing an onrush of pain that would change my life forever, but I noticed only my heavy breathing and sweaty hands. I turned back, pleading, to GP.

"Did that feel good?" He enquired.

"Look we can discuss this," I suggested, but he simply moved on.

"This is your dad. He beats you and enforces the rules. Crush him like an ant!" Came the imperative from GP.

"No, not my father," I pleaded. "Don't make me." With a trembling hand, I fearfully bought the hammer down softly with a little tap. I looked up guiltily. I knew this would not satisfy GP. "The monster won't like it," I whimpered. I snarled and brought my lips into a sneer for his benefit.

"Harder, smash him. Kick him in the guts!" GP insisted.
Dad had used that expression himself, mostly as a reference to starting machinery. I brought the mallet down a little harder, but only dented the wood. Sweat dripped from my brow. "Harder," GP urged. "Swat him like a fly." Like myself, GP seemed anxious, sweating and frenzied.

I knew it was only symbolic, but it was somehow more, as if I was upsetting Dad, or destroying family trust and the icon of what being a man meant to me. Years later as a teenager I would accidentally hit Dad on the top of his bald cranium as we were unloading bricks and it would bring back memories of when I was asked to destroy him, apparently for my own good. I hesitated with the mallet held high, wondering if he would know that I had betrayed him. I knew he would find out. I felt pressured as if I had no choice. I was growing addicted to the power. As the mallet began to fall with force, I realised I had to take responsibility for where it landed.

As the mallet fell, I glimpsed the monster leaving the barely lit room and retreating into the even darker checked maze of my subconscious that had not been explored. I had never seen him run before and it was quite comical. His body was in disproportion to his legs. His speed came from short awkward steps on the tips of his eight talons that were built for creating terror and hunting. It seemed he was floating on a cloud, but it was only the many minions at his feet, running with him creating the effect. I expected they would drop off along the journey. He was fleeing, desperate to get away. I knew he was returning to his lair, a place I had never been to. It was his place of safety and peace, where his black grotesque nesting roots had taken into my being like a cancer tumour, winding deeply and growing on me so that it was no longer possible to tell what was mine and what was his. He didn't think I would follow him. I knew if I let him go he would always be there, bringing me down, harbouring stigma, creating doubt and possibly controlling me like a puppet. I had given him shape when a toxic part of me had escaped. I knew I had to make myself whole. For the first time he had displayed fear and doubted himself. I wanted to meet him again and I knew I must. My very sanity depended on it. With my features set determinedly to complete the task, I breathed deeply and took the first steps in the pursuit.

As he ran through my subconscious memory, the landmarks were recognisable at first. He fled the city down the winding, tarred Albany Highway. I lost sight of him on the long journey, but I knew where he was taking me. I was in control now. I knew what I had created and what I must do. With a feeling of sinking dread, I would keep him as a shape in the distance. He led me through the dry summer days until, as the great storm arrived, I was in a place of conflict. He went to the school and The Big Boys' Playground, where he taunted me about my masculinity and laughed at my repetitions and social ineptitude, but I knew he could not hurt me if I didn't submit my will. I looked him squarely in the eye. I shuddered when I saw the bully and the toilet block where he had assaulted me and told me he had a knife. I glimpsed Sister Bernard in her classroom under her long white veil, ruling by fear, but did not falter as I heard GP's firm command through the fog. "These are your teachers. They torment you and give you work you can't do. Destroy them now!"

It was all I could do to smash hard. I thought of Sister Bernard and not Miss Noske, although I was angry at her for giving homework. Mostly, I thought of my sore and bleeding knuckles, my red ears, my broken nose and the laughter and humiliating looks from my peers. Now she was brittle and exposed. "You hate Sister Bernard! Keep smashing!" GP instructed loudly. The instruction reverberated off the walls and into my soul.

"God forgive me for smashing a nun," I proclaimed aloud, but I smashed until the wooden pieces were pulp. I smashed until her nose and every bone in her hands were shattered. I smashed until I was in a frenzy. I smashed until my anger and vengeance were gone and the chamfers became splinters. In the end there was nothing left but tears in my eyes.

GP kept going: "These are the faceless haters, the doctors who sent you here, your peers and bullies. I know you hate Cowan. I know you were bullied at school. Take them out like the zombies they are." Once again, I picked up the hammer.

Avoiding more confrontation, the monster left the town then. I saw and even felt under my feet the long dusty paddock tracks and the dry barren stubbles where he arrived at his penultimate destination. He slowed to take me to the scene of my accident, where he had made the short journey from his lair, and I had first encountered him. I was once again on the grassy hill next to the old red windmill. He paused to remind me of my mortality and my bargain with him. It was a bargain I had made under weakness and duress. I could sense his den was nearby. In the shrouded mist I saw the silhouettes of Dad and Uncle John dipping sheep and felt the peace of childhood.

He expected I would be fearful to go to the killing shed and the animal pens. He led me past the swirling whirlpool of the spirits of animals slaughtered by my father, that bleated and lowed, and dogs and pigs that walked on two legs in semi-darkness, skinned rams with horns and skeletons, shot snakes and crows. Dad had often made an example of crows and some were still hanging upside down. They pecked cruelly, but futilely at my eyes. He tempted me to ease my conscience and cease the chase with chores that had not been done, chickens that had not been fed, eggs that needed collecting and pleading yelps from starving pups. I thought the dogs were my friends, but these were not and didn't recognise me. I had fed, watered and cared for many dogs since they were puppies. Now in my moment of need they were repaying me with bared teeth, growling and snapping in rabid unison. I hesitated momentarily, aware of the longing to change things and assist, but continued on.

It was getting harder. Just as the monster was losing his minions, dead and dying parts of my resolve were falling off, to leave only the tempered steel underneath. I knew where his lair was. I had always known. It was in the shadows beyond the rusted barbed wire fence on the edge of the homestead. It was where I would stand sometimes and watch the final fingers of sunlight drag away the remnants of another day and shiver at the coming dusk. He lived in the disused well where a boy from a previous generation had lost his life. It was now crudely covered over by decrepit railway sleepers that protected it like guardians to a world of reincarnation.

Dad would never talk about what was under the sleepers and I was lucky to learn about it from Mum. I was sure in my own mind that the boy had been taken by the animals. I trembled with fear as I surmised that the monster was finding hope in the darkness and would use it to his advantage in the inevitable final meeting. I would be forced into the unknown, where there was no light, only mystery, movement and the sounds of beasts. Would my spirit be broken, or would the monster be crushed forever? The battle would be in his place of choosing near the uncleared scrub, a place of gnarled and knotted wood and lifeless silhouettes that I had never been in at night previously. Indeed, I had only ever run from it to find light and warmth. It was not the task for a boy. I told myself it was happening to someone else, someone braver, someone who believed they could win against the odds and face the terror of psychosis amongst strangers in an unfamiliar and controlled setting. I hoped for a glimmer of moonlight to be my friend. I shivered in the late winter air. I contemplated turning to run away as I always had, but sensed GP was somewhere behind me, threatening. I knew now there were worse things.

The monster did not reappear until the sun had well set. His voice came on the breeze, taunting me from a distance. "Do you know fear?" he goaded. "Do you know terror?" He had chosen the night well. It was moonless and starless. The low grey clouds cut out the silver strands I had longed for and rolled in to create a swirling greyness that was impossible to see through. I considered the nature of fear. I decided that fear was not really having a choice, or at least having to select the best option from two impossible scenarios, one not quite as bad as the other. I had made my choice and was determined to triumph. The moisture from the evening dew wet my shoes, but I took a first tentative step and then another. I had gone ten paces beyond the back fence when I froze. The logs were moving. The beasts were conspiring. A ghostly silhouette with long sharp horns, on what appeared to be two legs, hovered past, almost brushing against me, and then another. I swung around quickly, but faced only the nothingness of the stark night. I told myself they could not affect me unless I let them, but the stench of decaying flesh was very real. The bleating of sheep and the hooting of owls did just not seem right. Had they always been like that? I cursed GP then for the drugs he had given me. Had they helped or made things worse? My thoughts were addled and contrived, but I was conscious that at least I could still think them. That was important to me, even if it wasn't important to anyone else. It was almost as far back to the safety of the yard through the beasts. There was no turning back now.

The night breeze from the south ruffled my hair like an unseen hand. I looked for landmarks that would allow me to find the well in the distance. There were no stars, no moon, only darkness. *I must not get lost*, I thought, but in the mist I found my sense of direction failing. The prospect of wandering alone in the mist was unthinkable, even worse than what was motivating me in my quest. The goading of the monster seemed to echo from all directions at once. It pulsed inside my temples before returning to the blackness. It was almost with relief that I stumbled upon the thick sticky strands of webbing, from what I imagined was a hundred red back spiders. They caught in my shoes and trousers and retarded my progress, becoming thicker as I approached the sleepers outside the well. I tumbled over them, painfully banging my shin. It was just possible for a ten-year-old boy to move the large, but rotting, railway sleepers by themselves. I covered myself in dust and grime as I sank on my knees to lever them far enough apart to enter the round concrete perimeter. It took me several minutes to create a space wide enough before I stared down into the blackness. It seemed like the opening to oblivion. I knew I should not be here, in this place forbidden by my parents.

I knew it was wrong to move the sleepers, but the doors to my boyhood had to be closed. I thought tonight would be as good a time as ever. I wondered if I would be the second boy to lose their life in the gaping chasm; perhaps if I died, I would never be found. As I peered down into the well, it seemed even darker than the outside... or did it? I detected a hint of moving light. The distance was impossible to judge, but it had to be the laser-like eyes of the monster as its head bobbled. I slipped my waist through the space I had created, half expecting to have my torso torn away by savage jaws and cruelly barbed talons. I felt nauseous and had a sudden urge to urinate. I realised I had run it down.

I wasn't sure exactly how far the drop into darkness was, but if the glimpsed light was a guide, then it was not too far. Fully aware that it could be the end for me, I let go. My feet dropped over a metre. I landed painfully on my hip and was forced to sprawl in the dust like an animated cartoon character struggling for traction. The air in the well was foul, although the bottom was completely dry. I felt my way into the opening of a small cavern. I detected movement and just a dim light reflected from what I assumed was the monster's eyes. I saw him more clearly then. He seemed weak and broken by my victory over terror and my pursuit of him to his lair. His minions were no longer rallying to attack. I smelt his fear. It was to be an inglorious end to his dominion. In a final, desperate effort, he slashed at my face with his scythe like talons that made a long raking *razzzz* sound as they flashed close by. With a sense of freedom, I fully realised he only existed because I let him. He grew smaller. I felt his roots unscrew from my back and sag like a bloodied, shrivelled crucifix, that with a shrug off my shoulders, fell benignly at my feet. I shuddered at the fallen carcass, but like a steam train, hissing with relief as it approached its final station after a long journey, I was free.

The monster was finished.

My mind returned to other matters. The opening enlarged to a bigger space and then there was dim light. I felt a sense of calm. Was my ordeal ending? I had a moment of awakening as I realised I knew this place. I recognised the musty smell and the wide expanse of floor. I was back in the room!

I looked around. The mess in the room was like a bomb had gone off, or at the very least had been hit by cyclonic winds. My father and significant others had crumbled before my hammer. Their shattered remnants lay all over the floor. "How…? Why?" I muttered. The room had held my deepest fear after all. It had not been important that I had caught the monster, only that I had found the strength to confront it.

GP was looking anxious, but happy. "Now that's a job for the cleaners," he uttered in response to my rambling. "Good to see you're back with us. I lost you for a few minutes there. You seemed preoccupied. Were you with the monster?"

A few minutes, it had seemed like days. I was embarrassed that GP had witnessed my mental absence. "Yes, he took me on a chase, but it's done with now."

"Did you get the job done, Boss?" he asked.

I nodded, and gauging by his response, I had passed whatever it was that I was being tested on. I had become the judge, jury and executioner of my own demons. He put the long key back in his ring with a sharp click.

God's Own Country: Home 13 (September 1975)

I exalted in the throaty roar. The wind was rushing at my face and ruffling my clothes as I worked my way through the gears and put my new-found motorcycle riding skills into practice on the home paddock. I tried to remember what I had been taught from the brief instructions my older brother had given me. Rev the throttle, relax and into fourth, build up the revs, relax and into top, open the throttle completely and then bum up. I had quickly acquired the need for speed. To the casual observer, it wasn't all that quick, it was a farm bike after all, but to me it was if I was in control of a bright yellow bullet. I revved the throttle hard and the Yamaha, ever reliable, responded. I felt a sense of power and authority as the white indicator on the MPH instrument panel was forced more quickly towards the red and became frustrated when it would not move any higher. How fast could this thing go? I felt exhilaration surge through my body like a shot of adrenaline at the question. I kept my eyes on the flashing front wheel. Nobbled, worn, and covered with a green film, it slid and tore through the heavy spring pasture, flush with cake weed and moisture. Riding without a helmet made me feel like even more of a man. I noticed Simon in the distance indicating for me to put my head down to create a low silhouette like we had seen the best riders do in the Moto GPs on television. He figured that the slipstream would give an extra few miles per hour. It was a far cry from Phillip Island, but we were having fun.

The third term holidays had begun. I had been back only a few days. On this morning Simon and I had set up a "speed track" on a flat area of the home paddock where we felt we could attempt the land speed record in our 100CC bike. We had lobbied for the more powerful 175CC model that Uncle John and our cousins had, but were happy enough with what we ended up with. It was Simon's idea. The track ran from the homestead fence, up the slight incline to the old red mill and back. Sometimes we would time ourselves, or at least brag about who had hit the highest speed, always adding on a few miles per hour for good measure.

I saw the disused well flash past. Again and again I had ridden past it, confronting and beating it. I was revelling in my newfound strength and showing it who was boss. It was not as intimidating in the daytime as the sheep and cattle grazed contentedly around it in the warm spring sunshine. I felt embarrassed at what I had been afraid of. As I returned to Simon and the starting point where the flat section ended, the kelpies ran to meet me, tongues lolling, looking for a ride. I went back through the gears. The engine whined like a discontented infant before I rolled to a halt.

Perhaps Simon recognised my preoccupation with the disused well and commented on that when I had returned from a run.
"You know, Paul, that old well seems different somehow. It was always an object of terror when we were younger, with the stories about it and Mum worrying that we would fall in. Well, now it seems just another obstacle to go around. I guess we just grew up."

"Didn't someone die in it?" I asked. "The skeleton could still be there."

"That's what they say, although I don't really believe it myself." I grinned sardonically at Simon's words and shivered. He would never know the terror it held for me. I considered if he went to explore it on a freezing, moonless night, his perspective might change. "You know, we could probably remove those sleepers and have a look," he suggested. We both stared at each other blankly, waiting for the other to make the first move. I certainly wasn't going to. I felt that I had conquered my fear to a sufficient level for the time being. Riding your motorcycle quickly was one thing, but entering a crumbling and abandoned well to look for dead bodies was another. I was happy with my current victory.

After I came home for good, although it was holiday time, it had not been easy. My family looking at me strangely had been the least of my problems. Jenny noted that my personality had changed, and parts of my old spontaneity had been lost, or I concluded, beaten out of me. I had become an alien to the town and realised that the settling back in process would take some time. I felt I didn't fit into the country culture after being away in the city, even though I was "one of the boys" and fronted up for a new footy team. I enjoyed being in the team as I felt I could express myself in things I liked. It was good to get away from worrying about what others thought.

I was "that boy" and became self-conscious of being added on or attached to everyday events that I used to take for granted. It was as if I had forfeited my entitlements to be who I was and had to start again. GP had told me that people would be wary of the mental toughness of someone to come through what I had and continued to function. I knew there were people in the town who didn't like me, or didn't like my family. This polarised opinion even more. It was hard enough sometimes being a Catholic and attending a Catholic school. The pool of folks to look for support with was small. It was more difficult to support someone who had been to the "loony bin," but some people stood by me because of my nature. I had not realised that there were people that liked me in the town previously. Some continued to like me, but most made favourites of others, sometimes my own family members. As I went through the motions it became a case of, "Who was this new member of the Kain family?" Apparently, a rumour went around that I was a foster child, started by those who knew little of the background. Even my friends and classmates weren't sure how to take me. There was still unrest following the Sister Bernard incident, as I had to endure the stigma of living in a small town after being publicly and viciously beaten by a teacher. At the end of the day, she wasn't going anywhere. I lived in terror of her thick ruler and lashing tongue.

It was ironic in the extreme, but the first few nights back at home I actually missed the attentions of Miss Raatz at bedtime. It was fantastic to be back with my parents, but the new rules and routines took a little getting used to. "Are we going to play kiss chasey?" I naively asked my mother as she tucked me into bed. I wiped a tear from my eye. She looked at me strangely. "I'm very tired, darling, and we don't normally do that, do we?" she replied.

"Miss Raatz does," I continued unabated. "She took me to the movies. I sang to her." Mum tucked me in quickly and looked upset. A few minutes later, I heard Mum and Dad talking loudly in the kitchen and I caught a word I didn't know the meaning of. "What's a trollop?" I asked Simon before my eyes closed.

"I'll tell you tomorrow, now go to sleep will you," came the curt reply. All he could do when I asked him about it the next day was to blush. I found this surprising. Simon never blushed.

***

It was only a week after my therapy in the room that I left Stubbs. At last the powers that be seemed satisfied that the anger of their longest serving client had been appropriately expressed and I was "somewhat better." On paper, at least, the treatment had been effective and I was officially cured. I revelled in the small victories and the nice things that had been said about my progress, even though it was not really the way I had seen events. The system had been declared the winner, although it had been as without mercy as the monster. The following document was signed on my leaving:

Name: Paul Francis Kain
Age: 10
Length of stay (in weeks): 23 and 3 days
Date of Discharge: 22.8.75
Referral Problems: Obsessive compulsive state and school refusal.

Problems apparent in Hospital: Unable to mix with peer group, not aggressive, but uninterested and not prepared to make an effort. Obsessive behaviour Poor hygiene. Complained of stomach aches regularly and vomiting regularly (about once a fortnight). Anxiety especially on parents' departure at visitation or after W.E.L (weekends away) Poor eating habits and some mealtime behaviour problems. Dislike of women but unable to communicate this to family, some physical aggressive behaviour towards women, usually during rough and tumble. Inability to express feelings, especially anger.

Changes Effected: Paul has missed only two days of school due to a virus, he has shown no school refusal behaviour apart from initial anxiety, since admission to STH (Stubbs Terrace Hospital), interaction with peers improved as Paul was motivated to join in activities. Obsessive compulsive state now non-existent, insomniac complaints diminished, eating, and sleeping well now, still unable to express anger adequately. Dislike of women still exists, but not so intense now. Father still anxious re his family-based interaction Paul somewhat better.

Agency of Follow-up: Mr Peers to see parents OP
STH STAFF for Paul on visits

So there it was. Six turbulent months of my life, explained systematically on a page. It felt like I had devoted the entire year to getting that final paragraph written on the leaving summary. I had put an end to the notion that I would never leave institutions. Quietly, I was proud of my efforts, especially the statement that I was making an effort and fitting in. I left the hospital and resolved to be a more vocal and active person in the future.

Years later, as I accessed the document for the first time, I questioned in my own mind some of the points that were not fully explained or contradictory. For instance, how could I be "not aggressive" generally, but "aggressive towards women?" I also felt uncomfortable about "unable to express feelings, especially anger." Even today I am confused by what seemed almost an accusation: "dislike of women, but unable to communicate this to family." My propensity for psychological analysis as a ten-year-old must have been clearly lacking. Perhaps my dislike of women was a reflection of my father's attitudes? It was a heavy burden to carry for a ten-year-old and I consoled myself again with the words of *Invictus*. At the end of the day, I could not control people's perceptions, only how I dealt with them:

It matters not how strait the gate,
How charged with punishments the scroll.
I am the master of my fate:
I am the captain of my soul.

Not knowing at the time that she had been ungracious in the report writing, I said goodbye to Miss Raatz. I hesitated before asking the important question: "Because I've been here the longest does that mean I was the most loved?"

She replied, "Of course, honey," and gave me a big hug. It must have been Miss Raatz that I had been aggressive towards in rough and tumble. If I had known, I would have felt betrayed. I played my last game of soccer at lunchtime on the Friday and said goodbye to Tommy, who wished me good luck "and all" back with that nasty nun, and he went over a few techniques for head butting, "just in case" I got into trouble on the sporting field. Ms Noske was sad to see me go and said she would miss me.

When I first looked at my departure notes it did not mention the monster or the battles I had overcome, the bully or Sister Bernard. It also did not mention chickens, suffocating blood, fights in The Big Boys' Playground or recesses spent staring at toilet walls. "How could the psychiatrist really know?" I asked GP who took me by the arm and tousled my hair.

"It's okay, Boss, it can be our secret. You're ready for life now. Let's get you back to Sister Bernard and The Big Boys' Playground."

With my bag packed, I walked down the corridor and saw Skinny Minnie and Fat Cat going about their morning shift duties. I said goodbye and realised life would roll on here as before without me. I glanced uneasily at the side "treatment rooms," and shuddered at their effect in changing people who fell into their trap. It was good to be having my final interaction with the barrier doors by stepping the right way through them. My ordeal was over, but I wasn't naive enough to think that all was well.

I had looked forward to this day since I had first entered. I knew I had now cultivated the strength to cope and to take what the world could throw at me. I thought back to my initial distress and the indifferent attitude of the staff towards my suffering and wondered what the walls would say if they could speak. It was not something that you forget easily. I knew I would not be taking up the offer to come back for a visit. I stepped out confidently into the car park where Dad awaited me as he casually chatted to GP.

***

At the end of the day we mapped out the motorcycle raceway and spent most of our time trying it out, Simon dinked me to the old red windmill to collect the course markers. We paused for a moment as we walked over the red ant nests that we used to torment with long sticks when we had been much younger. We climbed to the top of the dry dam's bank, Simon still limping after dislocating his knee, and sat next to the rusted pump mechanism. Water had ceased to be pumped by it many years ago. Only a little of its identity remained. "It's good to have you back, bro," Simon said. I was frankly a bit shocked by this showing of male fraternity. Simon mostly followed the example of his father when expressing emotion.

"It's great to be back, Simon. I had to make a lot happen to get here you know," I replied. From the incline, we took in the fresh green colours caught in the rays of the setting sun and the smell of the season's newly cut hay. The farm stretched up the hill and disappeared in the shadows of dusk. Simon sighed and then spoke, an awed expression pulling at his features.

"God's own country, isn't it, Paul?" Conceding to his seniority, I nodded in agreement.

Epilogue: 40 Years Later

It was nearing the end of my monthly appointment in my therapist's rooms in Claremont, the upmarket locality in the western suburbs of Perth. He was meditating deeply with closed eyes. In the dim light, I focused on looking down through the upstairs window. I jealously viewed the throngs of contented people frequenting the shops on Bay View Terrace below, scene of the Claremont serial abductions in the '90s. I wondered where my life went wrong.

I contemplated that perhaps if I had of been more disposed towards my father and agriculture, or at least pretended to be, I would have inherited a farm like my brothers. My decision had been to be my own person and pursue a career in education, rather than be guilty of "being born with a silver spoon in my mouth." Putting all my eggs in one basket had left me doubly sad for some time. I would see Dad in my thoughts and prayers for years afterwards, but yet be left, it seemed, with no monetary assets from him to carry on into the future with. At least he had died the way he wanted, with his boots on at busy harvest time. His masculinity was beyond reproach to the end. Even though he had experienced a small stroke a few months before, Dad's indestructibility had made him like Zeus on Mount Olympus in the minds of his children; his death had been a bolt from the blue. Only Mum seemed to recognise his frailty, sending him off with a sandwich each harvest morning and making every effort to check on him, or remind the boys to do so. I closed my eyes and tried to put the thought to one side.

I was glad my contemplations were invaded by the relaxing aroma of lavender. I realised the meditation must be reaching a climax. It would soon be the end of another session in which my problems were not resolved. I would re-enter the rat race with anger gnawing at my insides. My adult self-seemed in some ways as restless and tormented as my ten-year-old alter ego and I much preferred seeing a younger person when I looked in the mirror. Perhaps I always expected too much of my therapist, but at least I was seeing him of my own volition. Society had moved on a little it seemed. My almost retired body had endured the full circle of marriage, career and parenthood. The buffeting of middle age and beyond was causing me to resort to childhood triggers of hope. I could possibly start again. I knew my brow was furrowed like my older father's. I was terrified of turning into him.

Hasser was sitting back in his recliner like a benevolent dictator, eyes closed in hypnosis, deciding what direction my life should take. The air conditioning pushed gently at his locks. I had worked in schools with Hasser. I knew he was about my age. He was short, genial and handsome. The baritone voice that resonated from his smiling features belied his size and was inflected with confidence and reassurance. I thought he bore an amazing resemblance to Robert Downey Junior. Try as I might my mind put a goatee beard and moustache on him. All I could see in front of me was Tony Stark AKA Iron Man. I knew I could not compete with him to be the coolest guy in the room. I had been seeing him on and off after the breakup of my twenty year marriage that had yielded two beautiful boys, while I "got back on my feet." That had been five years ago. I had since remarried, more or less on his advice that I move on.

"Okay, time's up. Just bring yourself out slowly," he said, changing his breathing pattern to cater for speech and turning on the overhead light. I stretched my extremities and began cautiously to focus my blinking. Light hit them with a sobering reminder of the present. I became conscious of where I was. As I readjusted, I shuddered. I decided that it was as good a situation as any to break the news.

"This will be my last session." I heard my voice dimly, from a distance and through memories of better times. I explained that I had accepted a severance package from the Education Department and been offered jobs in the eastern states.

Hasser expressed shock and looked at me aghast. His expression said, "Give me a scotch, I'm starving." I was taken aback by his response. Perhaps I was expecting more of the philosophy of Tony Stark. Why wasn't he standing on the table declaring: "Heroes are made by the path they choose not the powers they are graced with?"

I repeated my confession and elaborated by saying, "They asked me to rest a while after twenty five years." Each of those years passed in a flash before my eyes as I searched for a younger version of myself to continue the conversation. "I can't work for them for eighteen months, so I need to work for someone else." I could see Hasser's mind computing, calculating. He spoke at last. "They might be doing you a favour. Where are the jobs you're looking at?" It was a cue to immediately go into Jarvis mode. I needed to immerse myself in a fantasy world behind strong barriers.

"I tried the main state centres and couldn't get in, so I'm looking at positions in Alice Springs, would you believe, and Cairns."

"Both exquisite places."

At least he had given me that. The search for a younger, more magnetic self had helped. I was able to go on. "I like the idea of the oasis in the desert. It's somehow peaceful. When you finally arrive, it seems worth enduring the journey through the aridness, even if it's just for a nice contrast to all the desolate landscape. The grass on the other side of the fence is always greener, as they say."

"Something good results from every decision," Hasser replied.

"I'm trying to look on the bright side. Losing your job, after losing your wife and kids is like the perfect apocalypse. I can start on a whole new road, literally and metaphorically."

Hasser continued to seem a little beaten. His look was of a man that was not only losing a client but doing so at a time of their personal crisis. I attempted to relieve his suffering. "Perhaps I could keep the therapy going by writing about it. You know I was institutionalised unjustly for six months as a ten-year-old. I think there's a story there that people would want to hear."

"That's a great idea," Hasser responded, finding some enthusiasm. "Anything you write down is a terrific form of therapy." He went on. "If you write for five minutes every day, in a couple of years you'll have a book." It was my turn to look shocked. I gave a small laugh of incredulity. He was deadly serious. If I was sincere about writing a book I knew it would not be that simple. I agreed with him that it would probably be therapeutic. For a brief moment I felt the optimism of youth. I stood to shake his hand to conclude the session, and indeed, treatment. Through the window I thought I caught a glimpse of a dishevelled blonde boy, that could have been me forty years ago, wandering the streets of Claremont after school.

Upon leaving, I turned into the flow of busy afternoon traffic. Now it was just me, my story, and the long road across Australia. I set my jaw, determined I would take something from the session to go forward with. I went home and sat down at my computer to open a new file. I felt Dad's warm hand on the worn chip on my shoulder. I began to write:

"When I entered the sterile and life-sapping hospital for the first time, all I was thinking about was brightening up my day by watching the colour television and leaving early…"